# Frappe with
# Philippians

Advancing the Ministries of the Gospel
**AMG** *Publishers*

*God's Word to you is our highest calling.*

## SANDRA GLAHN

Coffee Cup Bible Studies
*Frappé with Philippians*

© 2009 by Sandra L. Glahn

Published by AMG Publishers. All Rights Reserved.

Published in association with the MacGregor Literary agency
2373 NW 185th Ave., Suite 165
Hillsboro, OR 97124

Third Printing, 2011

ISBN 10: 0-89957-396-7
ISBN 13: 978-089957396-0

Editing and Proofreading: Candy Arrington and Rick Steele
Interior Design: PerfecType, Nashville, Tennessee
Cover Design: Bryan Woodlief, Chattanooga, Tennessee

Printed in the United States of America
14 13 12 11 –CH– 6 5 4 3

# ACKNOWLEDGMENTS

Special thanks to:
- Gary, my love—for partnering with me in every way.
- Ken Mauger, Elliot Green, David Lowery, John Grassmick, and Dan Wallace—for laboring to teach me Greek. χαρὶ τω θεώ.
- Members of Biblical Studies Press (bible.org) and translators of the NET Bible—for your help, apart from which the Coffee Cup Bible Study series would have been impossible. Thank you for laboring without earthly compensation so others might grow in the Word. May God reward you in this life and in the next.
- Chip MacGregor—for representing me with enthusiasm and good humor.
- Virginia Swint—for being a faithful friend, a consistent prayer supporter, and a fine editor.
- Rick Steele and Candy Arrington of AMG—for your expertise in both the biblical text and in editing content.
- The women of Rowlett Bible Fellowship—for your fellowship in the gospel and for serving as a test group.
- Cec Murphey—for your generous investment in this ministry.
- Thanks also to my prayer team: Ann Grafe, Willis Grafe, Chris Havlock, Mike Justice, Terri Justice, Ann Knauss, Kelly Knauss, Reiko Kirstein, Jerry Lawrence, Martha McKibben, Beverly Lucas, Barbara Smith, Virginia Swint, Jeni Ward, and Lance Ward. And thanks to all who pray that God will use the Word through this series to change lives. You know who you are, and your contribution is not forgotten. May the Lord reward in public what you have done in secret.

# INTRODUCTION TO THE
# COFFEE CUP BIBLE STUDY SERIES

The precepts of the LORD are right, rejoicing the heart;
The commandment of the LORD is pure, enlightening the eyes.
(Psalms 19:8)

Congratulations! You have chosen wisely. By electing to study the Bible, you are choosing to spend time learning that which will rejoice the heart and enlighten the eyes.

And while any study in the Bible is time well spent, the Coffee Cup Bible Study series has some unique elements. So before we get started, let's consider some of them to help you maximize your study time.

*About Coffee.* You don't have to like coffee to use this series for regular Bible study. Tea works, too. So does milk. And water. Or nothing. But embrace the metaphor: Take a "coffee break"—a bit of "down" time, away from the routine, designed to refresh you. And you can imbibe alone, but you might enjoy it even more with a group. More about that coming up.

*Life Rhythms.* Most participants in Bible studies say they find it easier to keep up on weekdays than on the weekends, when the routine changes. So all Coffee Cup Bible Studies contain weekday Bible study questions that require active involvement, while the weekend segments consist of short, passive readings that draw application from the texts you've been studying. Still, the specified days as laid out here serve as mere suggestions. Some people prefer to attend a Bible study one day and follow a four-day-per-week study schedule along with weekend readings. Others prefer to take twice as long to get through the book, cutting each day's selection roughly in half. Adapt the structure of days to fit your own needs.

*Community.* While you can complete this study individually, consider going through it with a few others. If you don't already belong to a Bible study group, find some friends and start one. Or connect periodically with others who organize short-term online groups announced at www.soulpersuit.com. These vehicles give you opportunities to share what you're learning with a wider community and gain from their insights, too.

*Aesthetics.* At the author's web site (www.aspire2.com) in a section designed for the Coffee Cup series, you will find links to art that relates to each study. For this specific study you'll discover works by Rembrandt such as "St. Paul in Prison." You'll also find links to other studies in Philippians, recommended commentaries, and additional ideas and resources. The more senses you can engage in your interaction with God's truth, the better you will remember it, apply it, and enjoy it.

*Convenience.* Rather than turning in the Bible to find the references, you'll find the entire text for each day included in your Coffee Cup Bible Study book. While it's important to know our way around the Bible, the series is designed this way so you can stash it in a purse, diaper bag, briefcase or backpack to use on the subway, at a coffee shop, or in a doctor's waiting room.

Why does the Coffee Cup Series use the NET Bible translation? Accessible online from anywhere in the world, the NET (New English Translation) Bible is a modern translation from the ancient Greek, Hebrew, and Aramaic texts. A team of biblical language scholars volunteered their time to prepare it because they shared a vision to make the Bible available worldwide without the high cost of permissions usually required for using copyrighted materials. Any other translation, with the exception of the King James Version, would have made the cost of including the text prohibitive. Only through the generosity of the Biblical Studies Press and the NET Bible translators is this convenience possible. For more information on this ministry, go to www.bible.org.

*Sensitivity to time-and-culture considerations.* Many Bible studies skip what we call the theological step. That is, they start by guiding readers to observe and interpret the words written to the original audience (the exegetical step). But then they apply the words directly to a contemporary setting (the homiletical step). The result is sometimes misapplication. For example, they might conclude, "Paul told slaves to obey their *masters* so we need to obey our *employers*." Yet today's bosses don't own their employees nor do they usually share the same household. Employment is by mutual agreement; slavery is not. So we should probably use the voluntary "submit" rather than obligatory "obey" when referring to an employment context. In the Coffee Cup series, our aim is to be particularly sensitive to the audience to whom the author's mail was addressed but also work to take the crucial step of separating what was intended for a limited audience from that which is for all audiences for all time (obey masters/owners of people vs. respect those in authority).

*Sensitivity to genres.* Rather than crafting a series in which each study is laid out exactly like all the others, each Coffee Cup study is designed for exploring the genre category in which the Bible book was written—whether epistle, poetry, gospel, history, or narrative. So the way we study Philippians, an epistle or letter, differs from how we would study the compact poetry in Song of Songs or a narrative such as Judges. For this reason while the studies in the Coffee Cup series may have similar elements, no two will take the same approach.

*Selections for Memorization.* A Cuban pastor incarcerated in deplorable conditions for his faith afterward told my friend, "The Word of God was of great comfort. One Methodist pastor took a notebook and a pencil and wrote down all the Scripture that everyone knew by heart and recorded them for all of us to read the Word of God." In the absence of Bibles, the only access these prisoners had to God's Word was what they'd hidden in their hearts—treasure their captors could never take away. Whether we live where Christians endure persecution or we're tempted by apathy from materialism's pull, we need God's word in our hearts to help us stand strong in every situation. So each week you'll find verses to memorize.

Are you ready to explore Philippians? If so, fasten your seat belt and travel back in time with me to ancient Philippi, where our journey begins.

# INTRODUCTION TO
# FRAPPÉ WITH PHILIPPIANS

We begin our story in Macedonia—eastern Greece—in the fourth century before Christ. The area is rich in goldmines so the father of Alexander the Great, King Philip II of Macedon, capitalizes on that advantage and takes over the town, Crenides. Not surprisingly he renames it for himself as "Philippi."

Philippi sits near the head of the azure waters of the Aegean at the foot of a mountain on the northern border of a marshy plain. That plain separates the city from hills to the south. The site controls the passageway between Amphipolis—the district capital, about thirty miles away—and Neapolis, Philippi's seaport, eight miles away. These cities lie along what will become the *Via Egnatia*, the Roman road crossing Macedonia and leading to Rome. Because of its prime trade location and gold, Philippi is the perfect site for establishing a garrison. So Philip II sends citizens to occupy the city and secures it with fortifications. According to Aristotle's successor, Theophrastus, Philip II also has the marsh partially drained.

A few centuries later, in 167 B.C., the Romans divide the surrounding territory into four separate states. And after that we hear little about the city for more than a hundred years.

Then in 42 B.C., Brutus and Cassius assassinate Julius Caesar. Caesar's heirs—Octavian (later to become the famed Caesar Augustus) and Mark Antony—triumph over the two betrayers. The heirs fight the assassinators on the west plain of the city at the Battle of Philippi.

The victors then release some of their soldiers and colonize them at Philippi. After Octavian becomes "Caesar Agustus" he establishes more settlers there.

So in the midst of Greek Macedonia sits this little Roman colony that enjoys higher status in the empire than its neighboring cities. Only about one in three of Philippi's citizens is Roman, but the city's Latin-speaking minority Romans rule the Greek underclass and give Philippi its distinct Roman flavor.

When the Philippian territory is divided into squares of land and distributed among the colonists, it keeps its Macedonian walls. Two Rome-appointed military officers govern the town, and many Latin inscriptions testify to the city's prosperity.

Nearly a century passes. In Bethlehem, Jesus is born, and about thirty years later He dies and is resurrected. A couple of decades after that in the 50's A.D., Nero rules.

While spreading the gospel about Jesus to the Gentiles, an apostle named Paul finds himself on one of those trips where everything goes wrong. On his second missionary journey he falls sick in Galatia. Then he wants to go to Asia, but the door slams shut. So he sets out for Bithynia. The door slams again. So he and his companions, Silas and Timothy, strike out, this time heading for Troas near the coast. As they go, they still wonder what in the world their heavenly Father is up to.

Then while in Troas, Paul has a vision of a Macedonian man who pleads for his help. Finally some direction! Doors fly open and the band of brothers set sail under favorable conditions for Neapolis (Acts 16:11). From there they walk to Philippi to spread the gospel in what will later become Europe. Their eight-mile journey takes them by road over a 1,600-foot pass leading over the Symbolum mountain ridge before traversing the Philippian plain.

Upon entering any city to preach the gospel, these missionaries usually head straight for the synagogue on the Sabbath. Yet Philippi

> For an interesting historical look at life in the Roman Empire, check out the thirteen-part BBC mini-series, "I Claudius," starring Derek Jacobi. If your local library dos not have it, ask for it through interlibrary loan.

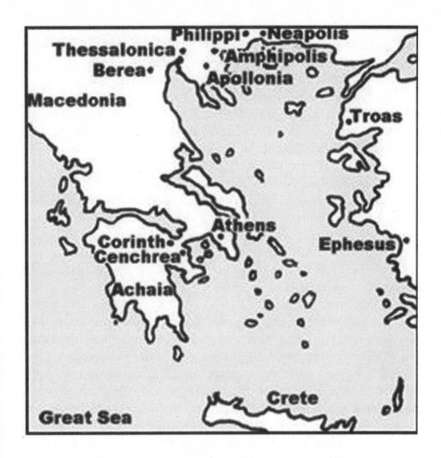

has no synagogue. So on Saturday they go instead to the Angites riverbank. (The riverbank was a common meeting place when fewer than
ten Jews met for worship.) There the men find some God-fearing
women—both Gentile converts to Judaism and Jewish women—who
gather weekly for worship.

The first person to believe in the gospel is a businesswoman named
Lydia. A seller of purple fabric, she's one of the Greeks from the city of
Thyatira, another city in Asia Minor (see Rev. 2:18–29). Thyatira has a
reputation for manufacturing purple wool fabric. Perhaps Lydia serves
in Philippi as the agent of the Thyatira Fabric Firm, or maybe she's
working independently, but her name suggests she's a freedwoman. (If
she's married, the writer of Acts does not mention her husband. Many
biblical scholars think she was a wealthy widow, as she is baptized with
"her" household, according to Acts 16:15.)

Immediately upon her conversion, Lydia extends hospitality to Paul and his companions telling them, "If you consider me to have believed in the Lord, come stay with me." She persuades them, so they reside in her home during the rest of their time in that city.

The men serve in partnership with Lydia and at least two other women—Euodia and Synthyche—contending for the faith. (In the account of Paul's ministry found in the Book of Acts, Dr. Luke records the events at Philippi using the first-person "I" and "we." So he's in Philippi, as well. Perhaps he even grew up there.)

The ministry in Philippi thrives. The believers grow. Paul and friends find their place of ministry—until a girl, a slave whose owners profit from her ability to predict the future, keeps following the missionaries and shouting about them. (Imagine trying to share your faith at the mall while someone follows you yelling, "These people are slaves of Jesus telling you how to be saved!") When Paul reaches his limit, he turns and commands the spirit to leave the girl in Jesus' name.

And the spirit obeys.

That's when the trouble begins. The girl's exploiters are outraged! No more fortune-telling means no more income. So they drag Paul and Silas before the city's magistrates and accuse the visitors of disturbing the peace and advocating law breaking. The marketplace riff-raff join in with heckling, so the magistrates strip Paul and Silas and have them flogged. Severely. Then the leaders send them off to prison.

As if being stripped publicly weren't shameful enough, flogging is utterly humiliating. And it never occurs to the city's leaders that their visitors might be Roman citizens with civil rights, perhaps because the companions of these men are predominately from the slave class. The jailer receives strict orders to guard Paul and Silas. So he throws them in a dark inner cell and fastens their feet in stocks.

Not only do the stocks hurt, but the wounds from their flogging throb, their stomachs nag them for food, and the stench of excrement nauseates them. (To our knowledge Philippian jailers didn't unshackle prisoners to let them "use the restroom.")

With Paul and Silas's ministry disrupted, their rights violated, and their bodies in pain, the men respond by praying and singing for hours while the other prisoners listen. Words and music offered to a mighty God reverberate off the prison walls well into the night. Everyone pays attention, including the jailer. Nothing like this has ever happened. Cursing? Yes. Singing and praying? Never. Eventually the jailer drifts off, lulled to sleep by the melodies.

Suddenly, about midnight, an earthquake rocks the building. Walls crumble, doors fly open, and chains fall loose. The jailer, jarred by crashing stones, sees moonlight through the roof and open doors and realizes he's virtually a dead man. Assuming his prisoners have escaped, he deems suicide better than the punishment for failing to do his job.

Yet Paul, seeing the glint of the jailer's sword in the moonlight, cries out, "Stop! We're all here. Don't harm yourself!"

The jailer calls for a torch and rushes in to find Paul and Silas with the rest of the prisoners. He can't believe his eyes. None have attempted escape.

Though thrilled, the jailer is now even more terrified. He trembles and falls before Paul and Silas. His countrymen worship Zeus, Apollo, Artemis and the emperor, but what kind of god causes earthquakes, breaks chains, and inspires prisoners to sing? And what kind of prisoner stays when he has the chance to flee? At first, this jailer feared his supervisors. Now he fears a God who can do such wonders!

Still shaking, he rises and leads Paul and Silas out of prison. And as they stand outside the rubble, he speaks with the respect he lacked when he brought them in. "Sirs," he begs, "What must I do to be saved?"

They offer a simple reply. "Believe in the Lord Jesus and you will be saved—you and your household."

So the jailer believes. And he takes the men to his nearby home. Once he has enough light available, he gets a good look at their wounds and sees the filth in their gashes. He washes them himself. Then he tells his astonished family and slaves about the night's events.

In the early morning hours, all the members of his household make their way to the river and are baptized, professing belief in the one who opens prison doors and sets captives free. Then they all share a meal thanks to the jailer's hospitality.

With the sun breaking above the horizon, Paul, Silas, and the jailer dutifully make their way back to the rubble-covered prison. Soon officers for the magistrates arrive. With their jail now in shambles, the officers announce that the magistrates want the jailer to release Paul and Silas and ask them to leave town. (Perhaps they hope Rome will never hear about the disturbance.)

Yet when the jailer tells Paul he's free to leave, the apostle delivers another surprise. "No way!" he insists. "They're not getting off that easy. They stripped and beat us in public without a trial, *even though we're Roman citizens.*"

The jailer's mouth falls agape. *Citizens!?* He wonders why that little detail hasn't come up until now. The men have been convicted and punished without a trial, a huge violation of law. The magistrates' superiors will be outraged when they find out.

"And they threw us into prison," Paul continues. "Now they want to get rid of us quietly? No. If they want us to leave, let them come and escort us themselves."

The officers deliver Paul's message to the magistrates. Upon hearing it, they tremble. And hoping to spare themselves, they rush to escort Paul and Silas from the prison.

Seeking to avoid further trouble, Paul and Silas agree to leave. But first they must go get Timothy and say goodbye to the rest of their friends. So they proceed to Lydia's house, where they encourage their brothers and sisters in the faith to stand firm. Then the three missionaries gather their few possessions and bid farewell to their concerned hostess and the little band of Christ-followers.

By noon the men start their journey, though Paul and Silas have already been up all night and are probably still in pain. This time they take the *Via Egnatia* and strike out for Thessalonica (Acts 16:38–40).

Before many days, the Philippian Christians send monetary gifts so the men can focus on spreading the good news rather than on merely surviving.

We have no idea exactly how long Paul, Silas, and Timothy stayed in Philippi. But we do know it was long enough to plant and strengthen a flourishing church for many days (Acts 16:18). The three men probably left Dr. Luke to continue teaching the flock, because Luke's account describing Paul's ministry in Acts changes from "we" to "he" until Acts 20:5, where we read that Paul returned to Philippi. Then the text notes "we" again.

Paul spent two full years in Ephesus before returning to Philippi. Then at the end of three months in Greece, his travel plans changed when a plot against his life was discovered, causing him to redirect his route back through Macedonia (Acts 20:3). So he made a stop in Philippi before crossing to Asia. There, no doubt, in the company of Lydia, Euodia, Syntyche, Clement, Luke, the jailor's family and others, he observed the Jewish days of unleavened bread. Then once again he told them all goodbye and sailed with Luke from the nearby seaport to Troas, where seven more of his friends awaited his arrival (Acts 20:4–6).

Paul may have paid one further visit to Philippi in his lifetime. He mentioned his hope to do so in his letter to the Philippians (Phil. 2:24). He also mentioned Philippi in his first letter to Timothy (probably sent to Ephesus—see 1 Tim. 1:3), in which Paul referenced a trip to Macedonia, which surely would have included a visit with his beloved Philippian church.

In addition to actually going to Philippi, Paul had relatively frequent correspondence with the church there. On two occasions the group sent him gifts (Phil 4:16). Later they did so again (2 Cor. 11:9; Phil. 4:15). After that, during Paul's first imprisonment in Rome, they sent a person—Epaphroditus (Phil. 2:25; 4:10,14–19)—with another monetary gift for Paul's support. Epaphroditus remained with Paul until a life-threatening illness made him want to return home (Phil. 2:27). And on this return, Epaphroditus carried a letter of thanks from Paul and Timothy back to their friends (Phil. 1:1). (It is this letter we will spend the next few weeks studying.)

By the time Paul wrote this epistle, he had heard of pressures on the church at Philippi from without. Yet even more disturbing was the word that his good friends and co-workers, Euodia and Syntyche, were engaged in a disagreement heated enough to threaten church unity.

As a letter-writer, Paul often had to compose difficult defenses of his ministry and faith. But not when it came to his Christian family in Philippi. To them he wrote his warmest epistle. And though he drafted this letter while under house arrest in Rome, he overflowed with joy. He loved them. And he was grateful to and for the Philippians for their continual support in every way. Not only did he rejoice because of his material gain through their generosity but more importantly because of what their giving spirit revealed about their spiritual health and the eternal rewards they would reap. Through the Book of Philippians, his thank-you letter for their financial gift, we see him thriving in hardship, filled with genuine affection for his coworkers, and as passionate as ever about the gospel of Jesus Christ. Now, all these centuries later, we, too, are the blessed recipients of that correspondence. For in it we glimpse the face of our wonderful, merciful Savior.

# CONTENTS

# WEEK ONE

## *United We Stand: Philippians 1:1–2*

The year was 1995. Bill Clinton was president. The Oklahoma City federal building bombing killed 169 persons. And O. J. Simpson faced trial for two murders. That same year our pastor, Dr. Bill, told his doctor he wanted to take a ministry team to Ecuador. Yet because Dr. Bill had a heart valve that couldn't handle high elevations, the sending agency redirected our team to a sea-level location in Mexico—to a city of about two million people called Culiacán.

So our team of about a dozen people arrived there to partner with a small church. And the on-site missionary, Tommy Beard, introduced us to Carlos, one of our translators. Carlos took vacation time from his job as the mayor's right-hand man to help us.

It didn't take long for everyone to love Carlos. He made us laugh, served us humbly, and had a passion for sharing the gospel. In fact he had already led many of the doctors and dentists he knew to Christ. He faced a huge obstacle, though. "I don't know how to prepare a simple Bible study, so how can I help them grow?" he asked.

1

Months later the mayor lost his bid for reelection, leaving Carlos without a job. So our church sponsored him for two months of summer school in Dallas. We enrolled him in a seminary class in Bible Study Methods, and our family had the privilege of hosting him in our home. On his third morning with us, I found him up early, sitting at the kitchen table waiting for me.

" 'Mom," he said, "we need to talk."

"What's wrong?"

"Nothing's wrong," his gentle Latino voice assured me. "I've just been up all night."

"Why?" I imagined taking graduate school classes in one's second language had to be tough. But that wasn't it. His answer surprised me.

"I've been in the backyard wrestling with God for most of the night. And I think the Lord is calling me to return this fall and go to seminary full-time."

I knew Carlos's unemployment left him with little more than a car back home. And the school's financial aid deadline had expired six months earlier. Additionally, he was nine months late for the fall-semester application deadline.

Still, we knew if God was in it, He'd make a way. So we dove into the application process and asked Tommy Beard to help us with the paperwork from Mexico.

Sure enough, within three months Carlos had finished summer school, landed a full-ride scholarship, and flown home to pack. He then drove from Culiacán to Dallas, arriving at our curb in his black sports car with everything he owned. When he pulled up, his already worn tires were bald, and the following morning two of them were flat! Having miraculously received a job offer in Dallas "just in the nick of time," Carlos was a walking testimony of the Lord's ability to "make a way when there seems to be no way."

Fast forward five years later to graduation day. Carlos received his diploma and accepted a senior pastor position with a church in a suburb of Dallas while he posted theological lessons by video on the Internet for his friends back home. Meanwhile, Tommy Beard was reassigned to a new city, and we eventually lost contact.

Five years into Carlos's ministry as a pastor, he agreed to add another responsibility—that of radio preacher. As the Spanish-speaking voice of Insight for Living in fourteen countries, his broadcasts suddenly reached millions. And less than a week after numerous stations in Mexico added Carlos's sermons to their programming,

Tommy Beard resurfaced. From his phone call, we learned the rest of the story.

Since we'd seen him, Tommy had served in two more cities in Mexico. And most recently his mission agency had reassigned him to a remote location several hundred miles from Mexico City where he knew hardly a soul. He was starting over in a new ministry and feeling a little lonely. Then one evening seeking some good Bible teaching, he turned on the radio.

And there hundreds of miles from Culiacán, he heard the voice of Carlos! The young man in whose life Tommy had invested—the guy who had once lacked the skills to write even a simple Bible study—was now encouraging Tommy in the Word of God.

Tommy found our number, picked up the phone, and called to tell us what God had done. Tommy had no idea that his faithful obedience would pay such enormous dividends.

And the Philippian women meeting to pray by the riverbank never imagined God would use them to found the first church in Europe. Or that God's eternal Word would record their generous partnership in ministry. Or that their faith would still touch millions of lives two thousand years later.

Are you "participating in the gospel"? Are you persevering in the faith? Are you investing in what lasts? Do you wonder if your sacrifice of time and money will make any difference? The One who sees all will reward deeds done in secret. God can make a way—and do so far beyond what we may ask or think.

Will you trust Him?

## MONDAY: THE STORY BEHIND THE LETTER

1. Read Luke's account of how the gospel first came to Philippi (Acts 16). Pay special attention to how Paul ended up there and what happened after he and his friends arrived.

> **Acts 16:1** [Paul] also came to Derbe and to Lystra. A disciple named Timothy was there, the son of a Jewish woman who was a believer, but whose father was a Greek. **16:2** The brothers in Lystra and Iconium spoke well of him. **16:3** Paul wanted Timothy to accompany him, and he took him and circumcised him because of the Jews who were in those places, for they all knew that his father was Greek. **16:4** As they went through the towns, they passed on

the decrees that had been decided on by the apostles and elders in Jerusalem for the Gentile believers to obey. **16:5** So the churches were being strengthened in the faith and were increasing in number every day.

**16:6** They went through the region of Phrygia and Galatia, having been prevented by the Holy Spirit from speaking the message in the province of Asia. **16:7** When they came to Mysia, they attempted to go into Bithynia, but the Spirit of Jesus did not allow them to do this, **16:8** so they passed through Mysia and went down to Troas. **16:9** A vision appeared to Paul during the night: A Macedonian man was standing there urging him, "Come over to Macedonia and help us!" **16:10** After Paul saw the vision, we attempted immediately to go over to Macedonia, concluding that God had called us to proclaim the good news to them.

**16:11** We put out to sea from Troas and sailed a straight course to Samothrace, the next day to Neapolis, **16:12** and from there to Philippi, which is a leading city of that district of Macedonia, a Roman colony. We stayed in this city for some days. **16:13** On the Sabbath day we went outside the city gate to the side of the river, where we thought there would be a place of prayer, and we sat down and began to speak to the women who had assembled there. **16:14** A woman named Lydia, a dealer in purple cloth from the city of Thyatira, a God-fearing woman, listened to us. The Lord opened her heart to respond to what Paul was saying. **16:15** After she and her household were baptized, she urged us, "If you consider me to be a believer in the Lord, come and stay in my house." And she persuaded us.

**16:16** Now as we were going to the place of prayer, a slave girl met us who had a spirit that enabled her to foretell the future by supernatural means. She brought her owners a great profit by fortune-telling. **16:17** She followed behind Paul and us and kept crying out, "These men are servants of the Most High God, who are proclaiming to you the way of salvation." **16:18** She continued to do this for many days. But Paul became greatly annoyed, and turned and said to the spirit, "I command you in the name of Jesus Christ to come out of her!" And it came out of her at once. **16:19** But when her owners saw their hope of profit was gone, they seized Paul and Silas and dragged them into the marketplace before the authorities. **16:20** When they had brought them before the magistrates, they said, "These men are throwing our city into confusion. They are Jews **16:21** and are advocating customs that are not lawful for us to accept or practice, since we are Romans."

**16:22** The crowd joined the attack against them, and the magistrates tore the clothes off Paul and Silas and ordered them to be beaten with rods. **16:23** After they had beaten them severely, they threw them into prison and commanded the jailer to guard them securely. **16:24** Receiving such orders, he threw them in the inner cell and fastened their feet in the stocks.

**16:25** About midnight Paul and Silas were praying and singing hymns to God, and the rest of the prisoners were listening to them. **16:26** Suddenly a great earthquake occurred, so that the foundations of the prison were shaken. Immediately all the doors flew open, and the bonds of all the prisoners came loose. **16:27** When the jailer woke up and saw the doors of the prison standing open, he drew his sword and was about to kill himself, because he assumed the prisoners had escaped. **16:28** But Paul called out loudly, "Do not harm yourself, for we are all here!" **16:29** Calling for lights, the jailer rushed in and fell down trembling at the feet of Paul and Silas. **16:30** Then he brought them outside and asked, "Sirs, what must I do to be saved?" **16:31** They replied, "Believe in the Lord Jesus and you will be saved, you and your household." **16:32** Then they spoke the word of the Lord to him, along with all those who were in his house. **16:33** At that hour of the night he took them and washed their wounds; then he and all his family were baptized right away. **16:34** The jailer brought them into his house and set food before them, and he rejoiced greatly that he had come to believe in God, together with his entire household. **16:35** At daybreak the magistrates sent their police officers, saying, "Release those men." **16:36** The jailer reported these words to Paul, saying, "The magistrates have sent orders to release you. So come out now and go in peace." **16:37** But Paul said to the police officers, "They had us beaten in public without a proper trial—even though we are Roman citizens—and they threw us in prison. And now they want to send us away secretly? Absolutely not! They themselves must come and escort us out!" **16:38** The police officers reported these words to the magistrates. They were frightened when they heard Paul and Silas were Roman citizens **16:39** and came and apologized to them. After they brought them out, they asked them repeatedly to leave the city. **16:40** When they came out of the prison, they entered Lydia's house, and when they saw the brothers, they encouraged them and then departed.

> The song "I Bless Your Name" includes reference to Paul and Silas's prison experience as told in this section of Acts.

2. What men were traveling together, assuming "we" means Luke was with them?

_____

_____

3. What do we learn about Philippi's geography and prominence as a city from the biblical account?

_____

_____

_____

Five years passed between the time Paul departed from Philippi and then returned. He made a brief stop there while on his third missionary journey (2 Cor. 2:13; Acts 20:4). Then probably another five years passed before he wrote his letter to the Philippians.

## TUESDAY: TESTIFY TO LOVE

1. Go back through yesterday's reading and list the people Paul and his friends encountered in Philippi. Summarize what happened with each.

_____

_____

_____

2. In the New Testament we find that churches met in the homes of women more often than in those of men [italics added by author for emphasis]:

**Acts 12:12** When Peter realized this, he went to *the house of Mary*, the mother of John Mark, where many people had gathered together and were praying.

**Acts 16:40** When they came out of the prison, they entered *Lydia's house*, and when they saw the brothers, they encouraged them and then departed.

**Col. 4:15** Give my greetings to the brothers and sisters who are in Laodicea and to *Nympha and the church that meets in her house*.

**Acts 16:14-15** One of those listening was a woman named *Lydia*, a dealer in purple cloth from the city of Thyatira, who was a worshiper of God. The Lord opened her heart to respond to Paul's message. When she and the members of her household were baptized, she invited us *to her home*.

3. After Lydia believed, she opened her home. When the jailer believed, he fed Paul and his cohorts. In what ways do you use your resources to show love for fellow believers? In what other ways can you do so?

Evidence suggests that when Paul wrote to the church at Philippi, he was under house arrest in Rome around AD 60. For the background on why he was imprisoned, we have Luke's account of events as they happened. Pray for insight from the Spirit and then read the first half, Acts 21:17–23:35. (To be continued tomorrow.)

**Acts 21:17** When we arrived in Jerusalem, the brothers welcomed us gladly. **21:18** The next day Paul went in with us to see James, and all the elders were there. **21:19** When Paul had greeted them, he began to explain in detail what God had done among the Gentiles through his ministry. **21:20** When they heard this, they praised God. Then they said to him, "You see, brother, how many thousands of Jews there are who have believed, and they are all ardent observers of the law. **21:21** They have been informed about you—that you teach all the Jews now living among the Gentiles to abandon Moses, telling them not to circumcise their children or live according to our customs. **21:22** What then should we do? They will no doubt hear that you have come. **21:23** So do what we tell you: We have four men who have taken a vow; **21:24** take them and purify yourself along with them and pay their expenses, so that they may have their heads shaved. Then everyone will know there is nothing in what they have been told about you, but that you yourself live in conformity with the law. **21:25** But regarding the Gentiles who have believed, we have written a letter, having decided that they should avoid meat that has been sacrificed to idols and blood and what has been strangled and sexual immorality."

**21:26** Then Paul took the men the next day, and after he had purified himself along with them, he went to the temple and gave notice of the completion of the days of purification, when the sacrifice would be offered for each of them. **21:27** When the seven days were almost over, the Jews from the province of Asia who had seen him in the temple area stirred up the whole crowd and seized him, **21:28** shouting, "Men of Israel, help! This is the man who teaches everyone everywhere against our people, our law, and this sanctuary! Furthermore he has brought Greeks into the inner courts of the temple and made this holy place ritually unclean!" **21:29** (For they had seen Trophimus the Ephesian in the city with him previously, and they assumed Paul had brought him into the inner temple courts.)

**21:30** The whole city was stirred up, and the people rushed together. They seized Paul and dragged him out of the temple courts, and immediately the doors were shut. **21:31** While they were trying to kill him, a report was sent up to the commanding officer of the cohort that all Jerusalem was in confusion. **21:32** He immediately took soldiers and centurions and ran down to the crowd. When they saw the commanding officer and the soldiers, they stopped beating Paul. **21:33** Then the commanding officer came up and arrested him and ordered him to be tied up with two chains; he then asked who he was and what he had done. **21:34** But some in the crowd shouted one thing, and others something else, and when the commanding officer was unable to find out the truth because of the disturbance, he ordered Paul to be brought into the barracks. **21:35** When he came to the steps, Paul had to be carried by the soldiers because of the violence of the mob, **21:36** for a crowd of people followed them, screaming, "Away with him!" **21:37** As Paul was about to be brought into the barracks, he said to the commanding officer, "May I say something to you?" The officer replied, "Do you know Greek? **21:38** Then you're not that Egyptian who started a rebellion and led the four thousand men of the 'Assassins' into the wilderness some time ago?"

**21:39** Paul answered, "I am a Jew from Tarsus in Cilicia, a citizen of an important city. Please allow me to speak to the people." **21:40** When the commanding officer had given him permission, Paul stood on the steps and gestured to the people with his hand. When they had become silent, he addressed them in Aramaic, **22:1** "Brothers and fathers, listen to my defense that I now make to you." **22:2** (When they heard that he was addressing them in Aramaic, they became even quieter.) **22:3** Then Paul said, "I am a Jew, born in Tarsus in Cilicia, but brought up in this city, educated with strictness under Gamaliel according to the law of our ancestors, and was zealous for God just as all of you are today. **22:4** I persecuted this Way even to the point of death, tying up both men and women and putting them in prison, **22:5** as both the high priest and the whole council of elders can testify about me. From them I also received letters to the brothers in Damascus, and I was on my way to make arrests there and bring the prisoners to Jerusalem to be punished. **22:6** As I was en route and near Damascus, about noon a very bright light from heaven suddenly flashed around me. **22:7** Then I fell to the ground and heard a voice saying to me, 'Saul, Saul, why are you persecuting me?' **22:8** I answered, 'Who are you, Lord?' He said to me, 'I am Jesus the Nazarene, whom you are persecuting.' **22:9** Those who were with me saw the light, but did not understand the voice of the one who was speaking to me. **22:10** So I asked,

'What should I do, Lord?' The Lord said to me, 'Get up and go to Damascus; there you will be told about everything that you have been designated to do.' **22:11** Since I could not see because of the brilliance of that light, I came to Damascus led by the hand of those who were with me.

**22:12** A man named Ananias, a devout man according to the law, well spoken of by all the Jews who live there, **22:13** came to me and stood beside me and said to me, 'Brother Saul, regain your sight!' And at that very moment I looked up and saw him.

**22:14** Then he said, 'The God of our ancestors has already chosen you to know his will, to see the Righteous One, and to hear a command from his mouth, **22:15** because you will be his witness to all people of what you have seen and heard. **22:16** And now what are you waiting for? Get up, be baptized, and have your sins washed away, calling on his name.' **22:17** When I returned to Jerusalem and was praying in the temple, I fell into a trance **22:18** and saw the Lord saying to me, 'Hurry and get out of Jerusalem quickly, because they will not accept your testimony about me.' **22:19** I replied, 'Lord, they themselves know that I imprisoned and beat those in the various synagogues who believed in you. **22:20** And when the blood of your witness Stephen was shed, I myself was standing nearby, approving, and guarding the cloaks of those who were killing him.' **22:21** Then he said to me, 'Go, because I will send you far away to the Gentiles.' "

**22:22** The crowd was listening to him until he said this. Then they raised their voices and shouted, "Away with this man from the earth! For he should not be allowed to live!"

**22:23** While they were screaming and throwing off their cloaks and tossing dust in the air, **22:24** the commanding officer ordered Paul to be brought back into the barracks. He told them to interrogate Paul by beating him with a lash so that he could find out the reason the crowd was shouting at Paul in this way. **22:25** When they had stretched him out for the lash, Paul said to the centurion standing nearby, "Is it legal for you to lash a man who is a Roman citizen without a proper trial?"

**22:26** When the centurion heard this, he went to the commanding officer and reported it, saying, "What are you about to do? For this man is a Roman citizen."

**22:27** So the commanding officer came and asked Paul, "Tell me, are you a Roman citizen?"

He replied, "Yes."

**22:28** The commanding officer answered, "I acquired this citizenship with a large sum of money."

"But I was even born a citizen," Paul replied.

**22:29** Then those who were about to interrogate him stayed away from him, and the commanding officer was frightened when he realized that Paul was a Roman citizen and that he had had him tied up.

> Paul replied, "Because I know that you have been a judge over this nation for many years, I confidently make my defense.

**22:30** The next day, because the commanding officer wanted to know the true reason Paul was being accused by the Jews, he released him and ordered the chief priests and the whole council to assemble. He then brought Paul down and had him stand before them.

**23:1** Paul looked directly at the council and said, "Brothers, I have lived my life with a clear conscience before God to this day."

**23:2** At that the high priest Ananias ordered those standing near Paul to strike him on the mouth.

**23:3** Then Paul said to him, "God is going to strike you, you whitewashed wall! Do you sit there judging me according to the law, and in violation of the law you order me to be struck?"

**23:4** Those standing near him said, "Do you dare insult God's high priest?"

**23:5** Paul replied, "I did not realize, brothers, that he was the high priest, for it is written, *'You must not speak evil about a ruler of your people.'*" **23:6** Then when Paul noticed that part of them were Sadducees and the others Pharisees, he shouted out in the council, "Brothers, I am a Pharisee, a son of Pharisees. I am on trial concerning the hope of the resurrection of the dead!"

**23:7** When he said this, an argument began between the Pharisees and the Sadducees, and the assembly was divided. **23:8** (For the Sadducees say there is no resurrection, or angel, or spirit, but the Pharisees acknowledge them all.)

**23:9** There was a great commotion, and some experts in the law from the party of the Pharisees stood up and protested strongly, "We find nothing wrong with this man. What if a spirit or an angel has spoken to him?"

**23:10** When the argument became so great the commanding officer feared that they would tear Paul to pieces, he ordered the detachment to go down, take him away from them by force, and bring him into the barracks.

**23:11** The following night the Lord stood near Paul and said, "Have courage, for just as you have testified about me in Jerusalem, so you must also testify in Rome."

**23:12** When morning came, the Jews formed a conspiracy and bound themselves with an oath not to eat or drink anything until they had killed Paul. **23:13** There were more than forty of them who formed this conspiracy. **23:14** They went to the chief priests and the elders and said, "We have bound ourselves with a solemn oath not to partake of anything until we have killed Paul. **23:15** So now you and the council request the commanding officer to bring him down to you, as if you were going to determine his case by conducting a more thorough inquiry. We are ready to kill him before he comes near this place."

**23:16** But when the son of Paul's sister heard about the ambush, he came and entered the barracks and told Paul.

**23:17** Paul called one of the centurions and said, "Take this young man to the commanding officer, for he has something to report to him."

**23:18** So the centurion took him and brought him to the commanding officer and said, "The prisoner Paul called me and asked me to bring this young man to you because he has something to tell you."

**23:19** The commanding officer took him by the hand, withdrew privately, and asked, "What is it that you want to report to me?"

**23:20** He replied, "The Jews have agreed to ask you to bring Paul down to the council tomorrow, as if they were going to inquire more thoroughly about him. **23:21** So do not let them persuade you to do this, because more than forty of them are lying in ambush for him. They have bound themselves with an oath not to eat or drink anything until they have killed him, and now they are ready, waiting for you to agree to their request."

**23:22** Then the commanding officer sent the young man away, directing him, "Tell no one that you have reported these things to me." **23:23** Then he summoned two of the centurions and said, "Make ready two hundred soldiers to go to Caesarea along with seventy horsemen and two hundred spearmen by nine o'clock tonight, **23:24** and provide mounts for Paul to ride so that he may be brought safely to Felix the governor." **23:25** He wrote a letter that went like this:

**23:26** Claudius Lysias to His Excellency Governor Felix, greetings. **23:27** This man was seized by the Jews and they were about to kill him, when I came up with the detachment and rescued him, because I had learned that he was a Roman citizen. **23:28** Since I wanted to know what charge they were accusing him of, I brought him down to their council. **23:29** I found he was accused with reference to controversial questions about their law, but no charge against him deserved death or imprisonment. **23:30** When I was informed there would be a plot against this man, I sent him to you at once, also ordering his accusers to state their charges against him before you.

**23:31** So the soldiers, in accordance with their orders, took Paul and brought him to Antipatris during the night. **23:32** The next day they let the horsemen go on with him, and they returned to the barracks. **23:33** When the horsemen came to Caesarea and delivered the letter to the governor, they also presented Paul to him. **23:34** When the governor had read the letter, he asked what province he was from. When he learned that he was from Cilicia, **23:35** he said, "I will give you a hearing when your accusers arrive too." Then he ordered that Paul be kept under guard in Herod's palace.

## WEDNESDAY: ALMOST PERSUADED

1. As you read the continuing account of why Paul is under arrest, pay special attention to how Paul's difficulties lead to the furtherance of the gospel. Pray for insight from the Spirit and then read Acts 24:1—28:30 as follows:

**24:1** After five days the high priest Ananias came down with some elders and an attorney named Tertullus, and they brought formal charges against Paul to the governor. **24:2** When Paul had been summoned, Tertullus began to accuse him, saying, "We have experienced a lengthy time of peace through your rule, and reforms are being made in this nation through your foresight. **24:3** Most excellent Felix, we acknowledge this everywhere and in every way with all gratitude. **24:4** But so that I may not delay you any further, I beg you to hear us briefly with your customary graciousness. **24:5** For we have found this man to be a troublemaker, one who stirs up riots among all the Jews throughout the world, and a ringleader of the sect of the Nazarenes. **24:6** He even tried to desecrate the temple, so we arrested him. **24:8** When you examine him yourself, you will be able to learn from him about all these things we are accusing him of doing." **24:9** The Jews also joined in the verbal attack, claiming that these things were true.

**24:10** When the governor gestured for him to speak, Paul replied, "Because I know that you have been a judge over this nation for many years, I confidently make my defense. **24:11** As you can verify for yourself, not more than twelve days ago I went up to Jerusalem to worship. **24:12** They did not find me arguing with anyone or stirring up a crowd in the temple courts or in the synagogues or throughout the city, **24:13** nor can they prove to you the things they are accusing me of doing. **24:14** But I confess this to you, that I worship the God of our ancestors according to the Way (which they call a sect), believing everything that is according to the law and that is written in the prophets. **24:15** I have a hope in God (a hope that these men themselves accept too) that there is going to be a resurrection of both the righteous and the unrighteous. **24:16** This is the reason I do my best to always have a clear conscience toward God and toward people. **24:17** After several years I came to bring to my people gifts for the poor and to present offerings, **24:18** which I was doing when they found me in the temple, ritually purified, without a crowd or a disturbance.

**24:19** But there are some Jews from the province of Asia who should be here before you and bring charges, if they have anything against me. **24:20** Or these men here should tell what crime they found me guilty of when I stood before the council, **24:21** other than this one thing I shouted out while I stood before them 'I am on trial before you today concerning the resurrection of the dead!'"

**24:22** Then Felix, who understood the facts concerning the Way more accurately, adjourned their hearing, saying, "When Lysias the commanding officer comes down, I will decide your case." **24:22** He ordered the centurion to guard Paul, but to let him have some freedom, and not to prevent any of his friends from meeting his needs.

**24:23** Some days later, when Felix arrived with his wife Drusilla, who was Jewish, he sent for Paul and heard him speak about faith in Christ Jesus. **24:24** While Paul was discussing right-eousness, self-control, and the coming judgment, Felix became frightened and said, "Go away for now, and when I have an opportunity, I will send for you." **24:25** At the same time he was also hoping that Paul would give him money, and for this reason he sent for Paul as often as possible and talked with him.

**24:26** After two years had passed, Porcius Festus succeeded Felix, and because he wanted to do the Jews a favor, Felix left Paul in prison.

**25:1** Now three days after Festus arrived in the province, he went up to Jerusalem from Caesarea. **25:2** So the chief priests and the most prominent men of the Jews brought formal charges against Paul to him. **25:3** Requesting him to do them a favor against Paul, they urged Festus to summon him to Jerusalem, planning an ambush to kill him along the way. **25:4** Then Festus replied that Paul was being kept at Caesarea, and he himself intended to go there shortly. **25:5** "So," he said, "let your leaders go down there with me, and if this man has done anything wrong, they may bring charges against him."

**25:6** After Festus had stayed not more than eight or ten days among them, he went down to Caesarea, and the next day he sat on the judgment seat and ordered Paul to be brought.

**25:7** When he arrived, the Jews who had come down from Jerusalem stood around him, bringing many serious charges that they were not able to prove. **25:8** Paul said in his defense, "I have committed no offense against the Jewish law or against the temple or against Caesar." **25:9** But Festus, wanting to do the Jews a favor, asked Paul, "Are you willing to go up to Jerusalem and be tried before me there on these charges?"

**25:10** Paul replied, "I am standing before Caesar's judgment seat, where I should be tried. I have done nothing wrong to the

Jews, as you also know very well. **25:11** If then I am in the wrong and have done anything that deserves death, I am not trying to escape dying, but if not one of their charges against me is true, no one can hand me over to them. I appeal to Caesar!"

**25:12** Then, after conferring with his council, Festus replied, "You have appealed to Caesar; to Caesar you will go!"

**25:13** After several days had passed, King Agrippa and Bernice arrived at Caesarea to pay their respects to Festus. **25:14** While they were staying there many days, Festus explained Paul's case to the king to get his opinion, saying, "There is a man left here as a prisoner by Felix. **25:15** When I was in Jerusalem, the chief priests and the elders of the Jews informed me about him, asking for a sentence of condemnation against him. **25:15** I answered them that it was not the custom of the Romans to hand over anyone before the accused had met his accusers face to face and had been given an opportunity to make a defense against the accusation. **25:16** So after they came back here with me, I did not postpone the case, but the next day I sat on the judgment seat and ordered the man to be brought. **25:17** When his accusers stood up, they did not charge him with any of the evil deeds I had suspected. **25:19** Rather they had several points of disagreement with him about their own religion and about a man named Jesus who was dead, whom Paul claimed to be alive. **25:20** Because I was at a loss how I could investigate these matters, I asked if he were willing to go to Jerusalem and be tried there on these charges. **25:21** But when Paul appealed to be kept in custody for the decision of His Majesty the Emperor, I ordered him to be kept under guard until I could send him to Caesar."

**25:22** Agrippa said to Festus, "I would also like to hear the man myself."

"Tomorrow," he replied, "you will hear him."

**25:23** So the next day Agrippa and Bernice came with great pomp and entered the audience hall, along with the senior military officers and the prominent men of the city. When Festus gave the order, Paul was brought in. **25:24** Then Festus said, "King Agrippa, and all you who are present here with us, you see this man about whom the entire Jewish populace petitioned me both in Jerusalem and here, shouting loudly that he ought not to live any longer. **25:25** But I found that he had done nothing that deserved death, and when he appealed to His Majesty the Emperor, I decided to send him. **25:26** But I have nothing definite to write to my lord about him. Therefore I have brought him before you all, and especially before you, King Agrippa, so that after this preliminary hearing I may have something to write. **25:27** For it seems unreasonable to me to send a prisoner without clearly indicating the charges against him."

**26:1** So Agrippa said to Paul, "You have permission to speak for yourself."

Then Paul held out his hand and began his defense: **26:2** "Regarding all the things I have been accused of by the Jews, King Agrippa, I consider myself fortunate that I am about to make my defense before you today, **26:3** because you are especially familiar with all the customs and controversial issues of the Jews. Therefore I ask you to listen to me patiently.

**26:4** Now all the Jews know the way I lived from my youth, spending my life from the beginning among my own people and in Jerusalem. **26:5** They know, because they have known me from time past, if they are willing to testify, that according to the strictest party of our religion, I lived as a Pharisee. **26:6** And now I stand here on trial because of my hope in the promise made by God to our ancestors, **26:7** a promise that our twelve tribes hope to attain as they earnestly serve God night and day. Concerning this hope the Jews are accusing me, Your Majesty! **26:8** Why do you people think it is unbelievable that God raises the dead? **26:9** Of course, I myself was convinced that it was necessary to do many things hostile to the name of Jesus the Nazarene. **26:10** And that is what I did in Jerusalem: Not only did I lock up many of the saints in prisons by the authority I received from the chief priests, but I also cast my vote against them when they were sentenced to death. **26:11** I punished them often in all the synagogues and tried to force them to blaspheme. Because I was so furiously enraged at them, I went to persecute them even in foreign cities.

**26:12** "While doing this very thing, as I was going to Damascus with authority and complete power from the chief priests, about noon along the road, Your Majesty, **26:13** I saw a light from heaven, brighter than the sun, shining everywhere around me and those traveling with me. **26:14** When we had all fallen to the ground, I heard a voice saying to me in Aramaic, 'Saul, Saul, why are you persecuting me? You are hurting yourself by kicking against the goads.'

**26:15** So I said, 'Who are you, Lord?' And the Lord replied, 'I am Jesus whom you are persecuting. **26:16** But get up and stand on your feet, for I have appeared to you for this reason, to designate you in advance as a servant and witness to the things you have seen and to the things in which I will appear to you. **26:17** I will rescue you from your own people and from the Gentiles, to whom I am sending you **26:18** to open their eyes so that they turn from darkness to light and from the power of Satan to God, so that they may receive forgiveness of sins and a share among those who are sanctified by faith in me.'

**26:19** "Therefore, King Agrippa, I was not disobedient to the heavenly vision, **26:20** but I declared to those in Damascus first, and then to those in Jerusalem and in all Judea, and to the Gentiles, that they should repent and turn to God, performing deeds consistent with repentance. **26:21** For this reason the Jews seized me in the temple courts and were trying to kill me. **26:22** I have experienced help from God to this day, and so I stand testifying to both small and great, saying nothing except what the prophets and Moses said was going to happen **26:23** that the Christ was to suffer and be the first to rise from the dead, to proclaim light both to our people and to the Gentiles."

**26:24** As Paul was saying these things in his defense, Festus exclaimed loudly, "You have lost your mind, Paul! Your great learning is driving you insane!"

**26:25** But Paul replied, "I have not lost my mind, most excellent Festus, but am speaking true and rational words. **26:26** For the king knows about these things, and I am speaking freely to him, because I cannot believe that any of these things has escaped his notice, for this was not done in a corner. **26:27** Do you believe the prophets, King Agrippa? I know that you believe."

**26:28** Agrippa said to Paul, "In such a short time are you persuading me to become a Christian?"

**26:29** Paul replied, "I pray to God that whether in a short or a long time not only you but also all those who are listening to me today could become such as I am, except for these chains."

**26:30** So the king got up, and with him the governor and Bernice and those sitting with them, **26:31** and as they were leaving they said to one another, "This man is not doing anything deserving death or imprisonment." **26:32** Agrippa said to Festus, "This man could have been released if he had not appealed to Caesar."

**27:1** When it was decided we would sail to Italy, they handed over Paul and some other prisoners to a centurion of the Augustan Cohort named Julius. **27:2** We went on board a ship from Adramyttium that was about to sail to various ports along the coast of the province of Asia and put out to sea, accompanied by Aristarchus, a Macedonian from Thessalonica. **27:3** The next day we put in at Sidon, and Julius, treating Paul kindly, allowed him to go to his friends so they could provide him with what he needed. **27:4** From there we put out to sea and sailed under the lee of Cyprus because the winds were against us. **27:5** After we had sailed across the open sea off Cilicia and Pamphylia, we put in at Myra in Lycia. **27:6** There the centurion found a ship from Alexandria sailing for Italy, and he put us aboard it. **27:7** We sailed slowly for many days and arrived with difficulty off Cnidus. Because the wind prevented us from going any farther, we sailed under the lee of Crete off Salmone. **27:8** With difficulty we sailed along the coast of Crete and came to a place called Fair Havens that was near the town of Lasea.

**27:9** Since considerable time had passed and the voyage was now dangerous because the fast was already over, Paul advised them, **27:10** "Men, I can see the voyage is going to end in disaster and great loss not only of the cargo and the ship, but also of our lives." **27:11** But the centurion was more convinced by the captain and the ship's owner than by what Paul said. **27:12** Because the harbor was not suitable to spend the winter in, the majority decided to put out to sea from there. They hoped that somehow they could reach Phoenix, a harbor of Crete facing southwest and northwest, and spend the winter there. **27:13** When a gentle south wind sprang up, they thought they could carry out their purpose, so they weighed anchor and sailed close along the coast of Crete. **27:14** Not long after this, a hurricane-force wind called the northeaster blew down from the island. **27:15** When the ship was caught in it and could not head into the wind, we gave way to it and were driven along. **27:16** As we ran under the lee of a small island called Cauda, we were able with difficulty to get the ship's boat under control. **27:17** After the crew had hoisted it aboard, they used supports to undergird the ship. Fearing they would run aground on the Syrtis, they lowered the sea anchor, thus letting themselves be driven along. **27:18** The next day, because we were violently battered by the storm, they began throwing the cargo overboard, **27:19** and on the third day they threw the ship's gear overboard with their own hands. **27:20** When neither sun nor stars appeared for many days and a violent storm continued to batter us, we finally abandoned all hope of being saved.

**27:21** Since many of them had no desire to eat, Paul stood up among them and said, "Men, you should have listened to me and not put out to sea from Crete, thus avoiding this damage and loss. **27:22** And now I advise you to keep up your courage, for there will be no loss of life among you, but only the ship will be lost. **27:23**

For last night an angel of the God to whom I belong and whom I serve came to me **27:24** and said, 'Do not be afraid, Paul! You must stand before Caesar, and God has graciously granted you the safety of all who are sailing with you.' **27:25** Therefore keep up your courage, men, for I have faith in God that it will be just as I have been told. **27:26** But we must run aground on some island."

**27:27** When the fourteenth night had come, while we were being driven across the Adriatic Sea, about midnight the sailors suspected they were approaching some land. **27:28** They took soundings and found the water was twenty fathoms deep; when they had sailed a little farther they took soundings again and found it was fifteen fathoms deep. **27:29** Because they were afraid that we would run aground on the rocky coast, they threw out four anchors from the stern and wished for day to appear. **27:30** Then when the sailors tried to escape from the ship and were lowering the ship's boat into the sea, pretending that they were going to put out anchors from the bow, **27:31** Paul said to the centurion and the soldiers, "Unless these men stay with the ship, you cannot be saved." **27:32** Then the soldiers cut the ropes of the ship's boat and let it drift away.

*Can you find the cities mentioned in this passage of Scripture on Google Earth?*

**27:33** As day was about to dawn, Paul urged them all to take some food, saying, "Today is the fourteenth day you have been in suspense and have gone without food; you have eaten nothing. **27:34** Therefore I urge you to take some food, for this is important for your survival. For not one of you will lose a hair from his head." **27:35** After he said this, Paul took bread and gave thanks to God in front of them all, broke it, and began to eat. **27:36** So all of them were encouraged and took food themselves. **27:37** (We were in all two hundred seventy-six persons on the ship.) **27:38** When they had eaten enough to be satisfied, they lightened the ship by throwing the wheat into the sea.

**27:39** When day came, they did not recognize the land, but they noticed a bay with a beach, where they decided to run the ship aground if they could. **27:40** So they slipped the anchors and left them in the sea, at the same time loosening the linkage that bound the steering oars together. Then they hoisted the foresail to the wind and steered toward the beach. **27:41** But they encountered a patch of crosscurrents and ran the ship aground; the bow stuck fast and could not be moved, but the stern was being broken up by the force of the waves. **27:42** Now the soldiers' plan was to kill the prisoners so that none of them would escape by swimming away. **27:43** But the centurion, wanting to save Paul's life, prevented them from carrying out their plan. He ordered those who could swim to jump overboard first and get to land, **27:44** and the rest were to follow, some on planks and some on pieces of the ship. And in this way all were brought safely to land.

**28:1** After we had safely reached shore, we learned that the island was called Malta. **28:2** The local inhabitants showed us extraordinary kindness, for they built a fire and welcomed us all because it had started to rain and was cold. **28:3** When Paul had gathered a bundle of brushwood and was putting it on the fire, a viper came out because of the heat and fastened itself on his hand. **28:4** When the local people saw the creature hanging from Paul's hand, they said to one another, "No doubt this man is a murderer! Although he has escaped from the sea, Justice herself has not allowed him to live!" **28:5** However, Paul shook the creature off into the fire and suffered no harm. **28:6** But they were expecting that he was going to swell up or suddenly drop dead. So after they had waited a long time and had seen nothing unusual happen to him, they changed their minds and said he was a god.

**28:7** Now in the region around that place were fields belonging to the chief official of the island, named Publius, who welcomed us and entertained us hospitably as guests for three days. **28:8** The father of Publius lay sick in bed, suffering from fever and dysentery. Paul went in to see him and after praying, placed his hands on him and healed him. **28:9** After this had happened, many of the people on the island who were sick also came and were healed. **28:10** They also bestowed many honors, and when we were preparing to sail, they gave us all the supplies we needed.

**28:11** After three months we put out to sea in an Alexandrian ship that had wintered at the island and had the "Heavenly Twins" as its figurehead. **28:12** We put in at Syracuse and stayed there three days. **28:13** From there we cast off and arrived at Rhegium, and after one day a south wind sprang up and on the second day we came to Puteoli. **28:14** There we found some brothers and were invited to stay with them seven days. And in this way we came to Rome. **28:15** The brothers from there, when they heard about us, came as far as the Forum of Appius and Three Taverns to meet us. When he saw them, Paul thanked God and took courage. **28:16** When we entered Rome, Paul was allowed to live by himself, with the soldier who was guarding him.

**28:17** After three days Paul called the local Jewish leaders together. When they had assembled, he said to them, "Brothers, although I had done nothing against our people or the customs of our ancestors, from Jerusalem I was handed over as a prisoner to the Romans. **28:18** When they had heard my case, they wanted to release me, because there was no basis for a death sentence against me. **28:19** But when the Jews objected, I was forced to appeal to Caesar—not that I had some charge to bring against my own people. **28:20** So for this reason I have asked to see you and speak with you, for I am bound with this chain because of the hope of Israel."

*"We would like to hear from you what you think, for regarding this sect we know that people everywhere speak against it."*

*Doesn't sound very easy for the Christians, does it?*

**28:21** They replied, "We have not received any letters from Judea concerning you, and none of the brothers who have come from there has reported or said anything bad about you. **28:22** But we want to hear what your views are, for we know that people everywhere are talking against this sect."

**28:23** They set a day to meet with him, and they came to him where he was staying in even greater numbers. From morning until evening he explained things to them, testifying about the kingdom of God and trying to convince them about Jesus from both the law of Moses and the prophets. **28:24** Some were convinced by what he said, but others refused to believe. **28:25** So they began to leave, unable to agree among themselves, after Paul made one last statement "The Holy Spirit spoke rightly to your ancestors through the prophet Isaiah when he said,

> **28:26** *'Go to this people and say,*
> *"You will keep on hearing, but will never understand,*
> *and you will keep on looking, but will never perceive.*
> **28:27** *For the heart of this people has become dull,*
> *and their ears are hard of hearing,*
> *and they have closed their eyes,*
> *so that they would not see with their eyes*
> *and hear with their ears*
> *and understand with their heart*
> *and turn, and I would heal them."'*

**28:28** "Therefore be advised that this salvation from God has been sent to the Gentiles; they will listen!"

**28:30** Paul lived there two whole years in his own rented quarters and welcomed all who came to him, **28:31** proclaiming the kingdom of God and teaching about the Lord Jesus Christ with complete boldness and without restriction.

## THURSDAY: THE LETTER ITSELF

As you learned from the reading, when Paul wrote what we now know as the Book of Philippians, he was under arrest awaiting the outcome of his appeal to Caesar.

Whereas today we incarcerate people long-term *after* we declare them guilty of a crime, in Paul's day governments held suspects *before* they came to trial (see Acts 5:17–40; 12:3–19). We have to lose some of our ideas about contemporary justice systems to understand something of Paul's prison situation.

First, the idea of "innocent until proven guilty" would have sounded almost comical to someone living in the Roman Empire. Their mentality was more like, "Where there's smoke, there's a fire." That is, if someone landed himself in prison, he probably did something wrong.

Second, while democratic justice systems emphasize the right to a "speedy trial," prisoners in New Testament times could remain incarcerated for years without knowing their charges or appearing before a judge (see Acts 21:27 to 26:32; 28:16–31).

Prisoners received no meal service, so they depended on friends and family for survival. And whereas contemporary North American prisons provide medicine, blankets, and necessities, first-century Roman prisons provided almost nothing. In the absence of outside help, a prisoner could starve or die of sickness. When the Christians in Philippi learned of Paul's arrest, they commissioned a brother named Epaphroditus to serve him, and they sent monetary gifts with Epaphroditus. In fact we find both the Philippian Christians and some believers in Colossae sending gifts (see Philem. 10–14). But the Philippians in particular cared for Paul in this way.

While tending to the apostle's needs, Epaphroditus fell sick and almost died (Phil. 2:25–27). After he recovered he longed to return home, and Paul, being sensitive to this, saw Epaphroditus's desire to depart as an excellent opportunity to send a letter. So the apostle drafted a warm, personal missive in which he assured the Philippians of his welfare and expressed gratitude for their gifts. Additionally, he encouraged them to seek unity and challenged them to stand strong in persecution. Having been thrown in prison in Philippi and sung his way out of the situation, he had plenty of credibility for encouraging the Christians there to trust God through difficult times.

2. Ask for the Holy Spirit's wisdom and insight. Then read the entire letter to the Philippians in one sitting. (It's shorter than a magazine article.) Pay particular attention to Paul's emphasis on their history together and on furthering the gospel.

> **1:1** From Paul and Timothy, slaves of Christ Jesus, to all the saints in Christ Jesus who are in Philippi, with the overseers and deacons. **1:2** Grace and peace to you from God our Father and the Lord Jesus Christ!
>
> **1:3** I thank my God every time I remember you. **1:4** I always pray with joy in my every prayer for all of you **1:5** because of your participation in the gospel from the first day until now. **1:6** For I am sure of this very thing, that the one who began a good work in you will perfect it until the day of Christ Jesus. **1:7** For it is right for me to think this about all of you, because I have you in my heart, since both in my imprisonment and in the defense and confirmation of the gospel all of you became partners in God's grace together with me. **1:8** For God is my witness that I long for all of you with the affection of Christ Jesus. **1:9** And I pray this, that your love may abound even more and more in knowledge and every kind of insight **1:10** so that you can decide what is best, and thus be sincere and blameless for the day of Christ, **1:11** filled with the fruit of right- eousness that comes through Jesus Christ to the glory and praise of God.
>
> **1:12** I want you to know, brothers and sisters, that my situa- tion has actually turned out to advance the gospel: **1:13** The whole imperial guard and everyone else knows that I am in prison for the sake of Christ, **1:14** and most of the brothers and sisters, having confidence in the Lord because of my imprisonment, now more than ever dare to speak the word fearlessly.
>
> **1:15** Some, to be sure, are preaching Christ from envy and rivalry, but others from goodwill. **1:16** The latter do so from love because they know that I am placed here for the defense of the gospel. **1:17** The former proclaim Christ from selfish ambition, not sincerely, because they think they can cause trouble for me in my imprisonment. **1:18** What is the result? Only that in every way,

whether in pretense or in truth, Christ is being proclaimed, and in this I rejoice.

Yes, and I will continue to rejoice, **1:19** for I know that this will turn out for my deliverance through your prayers and the help of the Spirit of Jesus Christ. **1:20** My confident hope is that I will in no way be ashamed but that with complete boldness, even now as always, Christ will be exalted in my body, whether I live or die. **1:21** For to me, living is Christ and dying is gain. **1:22** Now if I am to go on living in the body, this will mean productive work for me, yet I don't know which I prefer: **1:23** I feel torn between the two, because I have a desire to depart and be with Christ, which is better by far, **1:24** but it is more vital for your sake that I remain in the body. **1:25** And since I am sure of this, I know that I will remain and continue with all of you for the sake of your progress and joy in the faith, **1:26** so that what you can be proud of may increase because of me in Christ Jesus, when I come back to you.

**1:27** Only conduct yourselves in a manner worthy of the gospel of Christ so that—whether I come and see you or whether I remain absent—I should hear that you are standing firm in one spirit, with one mind, by contending side by side for the faith of the gospel, **1:28** and by not being intimidated in any way by your opponents. This is a sign of their destruction, but of your salvation—a sign which is from God. **1:29** For it has been granted to you not only to believe in Christ but also to suffer for him, **1:30** since you are encountering the same conflict that you saw me face and now hear that I am facing.

**2:1** Therefore, if there is any encouragement in Christ, any comfort provided by love, any fellowship in the Spirit, any affection or mercy, **2:2** complete my joy and be of the same mind, by having the same love, being united in spirit, and having one purpose. **2:3** Instead of being motivated by selfish ambition or vanity, each of you should, in humility, be moved to treat one another as more important than yourself. **2:4** Each of you should be concerned not only about your own interests, but about the interests of others as well. **2:5** You should have the same attitude toward one another that Christ Jesus had,

> **2:6** who though he existed in the form of God
> did not regard equality with God
> as something to be grasped,
> **2:7** but emptied himself
> by taking on the form of a slave,
> by looking like other men,

and by sharing in human nature.
**2:8** He humbled himself,
by becoming obedient to the point of death
—even death on a cross!
**2:9** As a result God exalted him
and gave him the name
that is above every name,
**2:10** so that at the name of Jesus
every knee will bow
—in heaven and on earth and under the earth—
**2:11** and every tongue confess
that Jesus Christ is Lord
to the glory of God the Father.

**2:12** So then, my dear friends, just as you have always obeyed, not only in my presence but even more in my absence, continue working out your salvation with awe and reverence, **2:13** for the one bringing forth in you both the desire and the effort—for the sake of his good pleasure—is God. **2:14** Do everything without grumbling or arguing, **2:15** so that you may be blameless and pure, children of God without blemish though you live in a crooked and perverse society, in which you shine as lights in the world **2:16** by holding on to the word of life so that on the day of Christ I will have a reason to boast that I did not run in vain nor labor in vain. **2:17** But even if I am being poured out like a drink offering on the sacrifice and service of your faith, I am glad and rejoice together with all of you. **2:18** And in the same way you also should be glad and rejoice together with me.

**2:19** Now I hope in the Lord Jesus to send Timothy to you soon, so that I too may be encouraged by hearing news about you. **2:20** For there is no one here like him who will readily demonstrate his deep concern for you. **2:21** Others are busy with their own concerns, not those of Jesus Christ. **2:22** But you know his qualifications, that like a son working with his father, he served with me in advancing the gospel. **2:23** So I hope to send him as soon as I know more about my situation, **2:24** though I am confident in the Lord that I too will be coming to see you soon.

**2:25** But for now I have considered it necessary to send Epaphroditus to you. For he is my brother, coworker and fellow soldier, and your messenger and minister to me in my need. **2:26** Indeed, he greatly missed all of you and was distressed because you heard that he had been ill. **2:27** In fact he became so ill that he nearly died. But God showed mercy to him—and not to him only, but also to me—

so that I would not have grief on top of grief. **2:28** Therefore I am all the more eager to send him, so that when you see him again you can rejoice and I can be free from anxiety. **2:29** So welcome him in the Lord with great joy, and honor people like him, **2:30** since it was because of the work of Christ that he almost died. He risked his life so that he could make up for your inability to serve me.

**3:1** Finally, my brothers and sisters, rejoice in the Lord! To write this again is no trouble to me, and it is a safeguard for you.

**3:2** Beware of the dogs, beware of the evil workers, beware of those who mutilate the flesh! **3:3** For we are the circumcision, the ones who worship by the Spirit of God, exult in Christ Jesus, and do not rely on human credentials **3:4**—though mine too are significant. If someone thinks he has good reasons to put confidence in human credentials, I have more: **3:5** I was circumcised on the eighth day, from the people of Israel and the tribe of Benjamin, a Hebrew of Hebrews. I lived according to the law as a Pharisee. **3:6** In my zeal for God I persecuted the church. According to the righteousness stipulated in the law I was blameless. **3:7** But these assets I have come to regard as liabilities because of Christ. **3:8** More than that, I now regard all things as liabilities compared to the far greater value of knowing Christ Jesus my Lord, for whom I have suffered the loss of all things—indeed, I regard them as dung!—that I may gain Christ, **3:9** and be found in him, not because I have my own right-eousness derived from the law, but because I have the righteousness that comes by way of Christ's faithfulness—a righteousness from God that is in fact based on Christ's faithfulness. **3:10** My aim is to know him, to experience the power of his resurrection, to share in his sufferings, and to be like him in his death, **3:11** and so, some-how, to attain to the resurrection from the dead.

**3:12** Not that I have already attained this—that is, I have not already been perfected—but I strive to lay hold of that for which Christ Jesus also laid hold of me. **3:13** Brothers and sisters, I do not consider myself to have attained this. Instead I am single-minded: Forgetting the things that are behind and reaching out for the things that are ahead, **3:14** with this goal in mind, I strive toward the prize of the upward call of God in Christ Jesus. **3:15** Therefore let those of us who are "perfect" embrace this point of view. If you think other-wise, God will reveal to you the error of your ways. **3:16** Nevertheless, let us live up to the standard that we have already attained.

**3:17** Be imitators of me, brothers and sisters, and watch care-fully those who are living this way, just as you have us as an exam-ple. **3:18** For many live, about whom I have often told you, and now, with tears, I tell you that they are the enemies of the cross of Christ. **3:19** Their end is destruction, their god is the belly, they exult in their shame, and they think about earthly things. **3:20** But our citizenship is in heaven—and we also await a savior from there, the Lord Jesus Christ, **3:21** who will transform these humble bodies of ours into the likeness of his glorious body by means of that power by which he is able to subject all things to himself.

**4:1** So then, my brothers and sisters, dear friends whom I long to see, my joy and crown, stand in the Lord in this way, my dear friends!

**4:2** I appeal to Euodia and to Syntyche to agree in the Lord. **4:3** Yes, I say also to you, true companion, help them. They have struggled together in the gospel ministry along with me and Clement and my other coworkers, whose names are in the book of life. **4:4** Rejoice in the Lord always. Again I say, rejoice! **4:5** Let everyone see your gentleness. The Lord is near! **4:6** Do not be anxious about anything. Instead, in every situation, through prayer and petition with thanksgiving, tell your requests to God. **4:7** And the peace of God that surpasses all understanding will guard your hearts and minds in Christ Jesus.

**4:8** Finally, brothers and sisters, whatever is true, whatever is worthy of respect, whatever is just, whatever is pure, whatever is lovely, whatever is commendable, if something is excellent or praiseworthy, think about these things. **4:9** And what you learned and received and heard and saw in me, do these things. And the God of peace will be with you.

**4:10** I have great joy in the Lord because now at last you have again expressed your concern for me. (Now I know you were concerned before but had no opportunity to do anything.) **4:11** I am not saying this because I am in need, for I have learned to be content in any circumstance. **4:12** I have experienced times of need and times of abundance. In any and every circumstance I have learned the secret of contentment, whether I go satisfied or hungry, have plenty or nothing. **4:13** I am able to do all things through the one who strengthens me. **4:14** Nevertheless, you did well to share with me in my trouble.

**4:15** And as you Philippians know, at the beginning of my gospel ministry, when I left Macedonia, no church shared with me in this matter of giving and receiving except you alone. **4:16** For even in Thessalonica on more than one occasion you sent something for my need. **4:17** I do not say this because I am seeking a gift.

Rather, I seek the credit that abounds to your account. **4:18** For I have received everything, and I have plenty. I have all I need because I received from Epaphroditus what you sent—a fragrant offering, an acceptable sacrifice, very pleasing to God. **4:19** And my God will supply your every need according to his glorious riches in Christ Jesus. **4:20** May glory be given to God our Father forever and ever. Amen.

**4:21** Give greetings to all the saints in Christ Jesus. The brothers with me here send greetings. **4:22** All the saints greet you, especially those who belong to Caesar's household. **4:23** The grace of the Lord Jesus Christ be with your spirit.

3. The Holy Spirit guided Paul to write this letter initially to the Philippians and secondarily to us. What words did the Spirit emphasize to you as you read God's Word?

_____

_____

_____

_____

## Friday: Salutations

Today we'll familiarize ourselves with the main characters in the Philippian story and then consider what profound truths Paul packs into one short salutation.

1. Pray for insight as you begin studying this book. Then read Philippians 1:1–2.

From Paul and Timothy, slaves of Christ Jesus, to all the saints in Christ Jesus who are in Philippi, with the overseers and deacons. Grace and peace to you from God our Father and the Lord Jesus Christ!

2. How does Paul describe himself and Timothy in the two verses above?

_____

_____

_____

"**Paul**" (1:1)—Initially called Saul, Paul was a native of Tarsus, a major city and former capital of the province of Cilicia in Asia Minor (now Turkey). The city's history goes back 7,000 years. Around the time of Christ, Tarsus was the scene of the romance between Mark Antony and Cleopatra.

Saul was of pure Jewish descent. We know nothing of his mother. His father was a Pharisee (Acts 23:6) and from him Saul received his Roman citizenship (22:28). Saul was of the tribe of Benjamin (Phil. 3:5), and it has been said that he was born in the second year after the birth of Jesus.[1] Sometime around age thirteen, he went to Jerusalem to study under Gamaliel, a distinguished Jewish teacher (Acts 22:3).

A tentmaker by trade, Saul was a Roman citizen and as such would have been considered among the aristocracy in any provisional town. At one time he had a reputation for hating Christians, standing by as a bloodthirsty crowd in Jerusalem stoned Stephen to death (see Acts 7–8). Yet God miraculously appeared to Saul while he was traveling on the road to Damascus, and he believed in Jesus as Christ. Following his conversion (and subsequent name change), Paul preached Christ in the synagogues and lived Christ in the streets, gaining a reputation as a giant in the Christian faith. An apostle, he took the good news about Jesus to the Gentiles, facing rage from the Jews. He was arrested and punished numerous times for that reason.

When he wrote Philippians, Paul was about sixty years old in an era when a man's life expectancy was fifty to fifty-five. While we don't know how or when Paul died, many historians think he and Peter were martyred the same day. Many think Paul was beheaded in Rome during Nero's rule.

---

[1] _Unger's Bible Dictionary_, 831.

"**Timothy**" (1:1)—We see Timothy first mentioned in the Bible during Paul's second visit to Lystra (Acts 16:1-2). Paul took him as a companion (Acts 16:3), and personally circumcised him so that he might be accepted by the Jews. (Timothy's mother was Jewish.) Timothy was ordained (1 Tim. 4:14) and went with Paul on his missionary journey through Phyrgia, Galatia, Mysia, Troas, Philippi, and Berea (see Acts 17) as well as to Corinth (Acts 18:5). Paul spoke highly of the faith of Timothy's mother, Eunice, and grandmother, Lois, who taught Timothy the Scriptures from childhood. We know little about Timothy's father—only that he was a Greek (Acts 16:1).

> If you love to read historical fiction, check out Walter Wangerin's Paul: A Novel. It combines what we know about Saul/Paul and reintroduces him through several points of view: Priscilla, who meets him in Corinth; Barnabas, Timothy, and Titus, his companions; James and Peter, the "pillars" of the faith; and Seneca, the Roman writer, statesman, and adviser to Nero.

Timothy ministered with Paul in Macedonia and helped establish the churches there and in Achaia as well (compare Acts 16:3; 17:15; 18:5; 20:4). Paul sent Timothy to work with the difficult Corinthians, calling him his son whom he loved (1 Cor. 4:17). We see Timothy serving beside Paul in Corinth (2 Cor. 1:19) and certainly also at Philippi.

According to church tradition, in AD 65, Paul ordained Timothy as bishop of Ephesus, where he served for fifteen years. About the time he turned eighty, Timothy tried to halt an Ephesian pagan idol procession (these were common) and in response to his preaching, the angry crowd beat him, dragged him, and stoned him to death.

**Silas** (Acts 16:19)—Most scholars consider the Silas we find in Acts is to be the Silvanus we find in the epistles. We know he was a Roman citizen because Paul says "we" when describing how he and his companion, being Roman citizens, were mistreated (Acts 16:37). Silas accompanied Paul on most of the second missionary journey (Acts 15 through 18).

When a major council of Christian leaders under James in Jerusalem ("The Jerusalem Council") decided *not* to require circumcision of Gentile believers, Silas and Judas Barsabas were appointed—along with Paul and Barnabas—to convey the verdict to the churches in Antioch, Syria, and Cilicia. Acts 15 reports that upon their arrival at Antioch, Judas and Silas "being themselves also prophets, exhorted the brethren with many words, and confirmed them."

From there, the details about Silas get sketchy. Perhaps he remained in Antioch; maybe he returned to Jerusalem. But when Paul and Barnabas had a disagreement about whether John Mark should accompany them further, Paul chose Silas as his partner and Barnabas opted to give John Mark another chance. Then Paul and Silas, "after being commended by the brethren [at Antioch] to the grace of the Lord," proceeded on their journey (Acts 15:33). They passed a number of cities, strengthening churches and delivering the decree of the Jerusalem Council.

Timothy joined them along the way, and the team eventually reached Troas (Acts 15:41 through 16:8). Luke probably linked up with them there. At that point Paul received his vision about going to Macedonia, and they all went to Philippi. There Silas and Paul were thrown in prison together and later, together with Timothy, were escorted out of town.

Assuming Silas is Silvanus, he later received mention as having preached Christ among the Corinthians (2 Cor. 1:19; cp. Acts 18:5). In 1 Thess. 1:1 and 2 Thess. 1:1, we find the same three men—Paul, Timothy, and Silvanus—sending greetings to the church at Thessalonica (compare Acts 17:1–9). Silas also receives mention as a "faithful brother" and the bearer of the epistle of First Peter to the churches to whom it was intended (1 Pet. 5:12).

**Luke**—In the New Testament we find Paul—and only Paul— mentioning Luke three times (Col. 4:14; 2 Tim. 4:11; Philem. 1:24). Luke refrains from mentioning his own name in his works (The Gospel of Luke and its sequel, the Acts of the Apostles), which is probably typical of the style of the day. (In the Gospel of John, John omits his own name, as well.) Paul distinguishes Luke from Aristarchus, Mark, and Justus, who are "of the circumcision" (Col. 4:14), making Epaphras, Luke, and Demas the Gentiles in the group. Some early Christian writers believed Luke converted directly from paganism to Christianity, but we have no way of verifying this.

Luke first receives mention as part of the "we" who join Paul at Troas. He stays behind in Philippi when Paul and Silas leave, and he joins up with the missionary team again when they pass back through Macedonia (Acts 20:6).

Because Luke's introduction to the Gospel of Luke follows the classic format (see Luke 1:1–4), we know he was schooled to write in the cultured Greek literary style, a style equaled in the New Testament only in the Book of Hebrews. From this we conclude that he received a good education.

Paul describes Luke as the "beloved physician" (Col. 4:14), and we find Greek medical terms in his writings. Luke probably ministered continuously to Paul's physical needs. Once Luke and Paul join up, we see them as companions throughout the rest of Paul's life. In fact during Paul's second Roman imprisonment only Luke is with him (2 Tim. 4:11).

3. Note how Paul usually begins his letters:

**1 Corinthians 1:1**— From Paul, called to be an apostle of Christ Jesus by the will of God, and Sosthenes, our brother

**2 Corinthians 1:1**— From Paul, an apostle of Christ Jesus by the will of God, and Timothy our brother, to the church of God that is in Corinth, with all the saints who are in all Achaia

**Galatians 1:1**— From Paul, an apostle (not from men, nor by human agency, but by Jesus Christ and God the Father who raised him from the dead)

**Ephesians 1:1**— From Paul, an apostle of Christ Jesus by the will of God, to the saints [in Ephesus], the faithful in Christ Jesus.

**Colossians 1:1**— From Paul, an apostle of Christ Jesus by the will of God, and Timothy our brother

**1 Timothy 1:1**— From Paul, an apostle of Christ Jesus by the command of God our Savior and of Christ Jesus our hope

**Philippians 1:1–2** From Paul and Timothy, slaves of Christ Jesus, to all the saints in Christ Jesus who are in Philippi, with the overseers and deacons. Grace and peace to you from God our Father and the Lord Jesus Christ!

How does the introduction to Paul's letter to the Philippians differ from his other salutations?

4. What do you think the different introduction in Philippians suggests about Paul's relationship with the believers in Philippi?

_____

_____

_____

**"Slaves of Christ Jesus"** (1:1)—In first-century Rome, if a slave gave birth, her child was also a slave. Prisoners of war were often sold into slavery, and someone could become a slave through debt, too. That is, a debtor could sell one's self and/or one's children into slavery as payment.

Yet not all slaves had a low standard of living, nor were they necessarily uneducated. Certainly those doing manual labor could suffer under difficult taskmasters. But for the slaves of high-ranking officials such as senators and emperors, the life of a slave might come with luxury, authority, and interesting work (see Rom. 16:23; Phil. 4:22). Slaves could save money and own property, which meant, oddly enough, that sometimes slaves owned slaves.

Note other places where Paul employed the language of slavery to describe his relationship with Christ:

**Rom. 1:1** From Paul, a **slave** of Christ Jesus, called to be an apostle, set apart for the gospel of God.

**1 Cor. 7:21-23** Were you called as a **slave**? Do not worry about it. But if indeed you are able to be free, make the most of the opportunity. For the one who was called in the Lord as a slave is the Lord's freedman. In the same way, the one who was called as a free person is Christ's slave. You were bought with a price. Do not become slaves of men

**Gal. 1:10**    Am I now trying to gain the approval of people, or of God? Or am I trying to please people? If I were still trying to please people, I would not be a **slave** of Christ!

5. What do you think it meant to Paul to be a slave of Christ?

_____

_____

_____

6. Are you a slave of Christ? If so, why? If not, why not?

_____

_____

_____

"**To all the saints**" (1:1)—The word "saint" brings to mind the image of a super-spiritual famous person, perhaps wearing a robe, with a special title. Think of St. Christopher and St. Patrick and Saint Nick. Or women such as St. Mary, St. Joan of Arc, and St. Teresa of Avila. But true saints are more ordinary than that. New Testament writers used the word to refer to all who have believed in Christ. It simply means "set-apart ones." Christ-followers are set apart in service to Him.

7. Think of your friends in Christ. Each of them, according to Paul's usage, is a saint. What are their names? Saint Emily? Saint Michelle? Saint Jonathan? List some of the saints in your life. Are you a saint?

_____

_____

_____

8. Notice Paul's emphasis in Philippians on including *all* the saints:

> **1:4** Always in my every prayer for **all of you** I pray with joy

> **1:7** For it is right for me to think this about **all of you**, because I have you in my heart, since both in my imprisonment and in the defense and confirmation of the gospel **all of you** became partners together with me in the grace of God.

> **1:8** For God is my witness that I long for **all of you** with the affection of Christ Jesus.

> **1:25** And since I am sure of this, I know that I will remain and continue with **all of you** for the sake of your progress and joy in the faith,

> **2:17** But even if I am being poured out like a drink-offering on the sacrifice and service of your faith, I have joy and rejoice together with **all of you**.

> **2:26** Indeed, he greatly missed **all of you** and was distressed because you heard that he had been ill.

> **4:21** Give greetings to **all the saints** in Christ Jesus.

Why do you think he placed such an emphasis on everybody, rather than directing his letter to "those in charge"?

_____

_____

_____

**"In Christ Jesus"** (1:1)—Paul likes the phrase, "in Jesus Christ" or "in Christ Jesus," using it often in his writings. Here he probably intended his readers to think of themselves as joined to Christ, the author of a new "race" of people. The Philippians had been made members of Christ's lineage by faith.

**"Overseers and deacons"** (1:1)—Paul seems to go out of his way to avoid authority or power terms (not even tacking on a suffix such as we often do with "servant-leader") to refer to those responsible for the care of the church flock. Though it's difficult to say with certainty, a survey of Paul's use of the terms elsewhere suggests "overseers" seemed to be those who care for people's spiritual needs and "deacons" were those who handled administrative tasks such as money-handling and delivery associated with meeting physical needs. Assuming the titles referred to church offices, those who held them probably had to maintain a high standard of Christian character (see 1 Tim. 3:1–7).

9. To whom did Paul address his epistle (1:2)? What does the number implied in "overseers and deacons" tell us about the organizational structure in the church at Philippi?

\
\
\

10. As noted, the terms Paul used to describe himself and those who cared for the church included "slave," "deacon" (which is Greek for *servant*), and "overseer." He didn't call himself "head-honcho," nor did he call those with responsibility for spiritual oversight "the ones in charge" or even "leaders." Not even "servant-leaders." Why do you think he choses such humble terms?

\
\
\

"**Grace and peace**" (1:2)—We'll explore these terms in depth tomorrow.

## SATURDAY: ALOHA, Y'ALL!

I must begin with a confession. I used to think the word "sensibility" was a form of the word "sensible." They sound similar, right? Only after I took a literature class in my PhD program and overheard some students discussing the sisters in Jane Austen's book, *Sense and Sensibility*, did I realize the words had nearly opposite meanings. In Austen's story one sister is sensible, on the extreme end of reserved.

The other has a wildly fluctuating capacity for sensation or emotion—sensibility—wearing all her feelings on her lovely, nineteenth-century detachtable sleeve.

I found this revelation of my ignorance particularly embarrassing because I have seen the movie adapted from Austen's book at least seven times. And if my sister called me tonight to invite me for another viewing, I'd cancel everything and show up in jammies holding a mug of mocha. Bring on *anything* Austen (preferably in a six-hour BBC format), and I'm there.

Interestingly enough, that selfsame story and my misunderstanding about its title helped me see something Paul wants to emphasize in his greeting to the Philippians. On first glance his words seem like standard epistle fare: "Grace to you and peace from God our Father and the Lord Jesus Christ." Sounds like a typical Pauline greeting, a long synonym for "Dear Philippians . . ."

Yet actually, in his short, standard-sounding introductory phrase, we find an entire sermon on unity. His readers would have picked right up on it, too.

Allow me to explain. As you probably know, in *Sense and Sensibility* the sisters refer to each other as "dearest." Consequently, some of my friends and I no longer use "dear" in our written greetings to each other. Where I used to write the usual, "Dear Virginia," or "Dear Eva," I now write "Dear*est* Virginia" and "Eva dearest." In return, I sometimes receive letters that begin "Dearest Sandi" or simply "Dearest." The minor change in wording completely changes the meaning, doesn't it? The words still follow typical formatting and they sound much like the original salutation, yet the addition (or deletion) of a few letters expresses a more affectionate tone. The small changes make quite a difference—in the same way a minor shift in letters differentiates the meanings of *sense* and *sensibility*.

We see in Paul's writing something similar. When he wrote to the Philippians, the typical Greek salutation was the verb, *chairein,* or "rejoice!" Yet he chose to use a different word with the same root—a noun, *charis,* or grace. And in doing so he pointed to the ultimate *cause* for rejoicing: God's blessing with no-strings-attached favor. Paul's greeting is a blessing, then, like a prayer for the lives of the believers in Philippi to be filled with God's undeserved kindness.

Yet the apostle didn't stop there. He also added the Jewish idea of *shalom:* peace.

By combining *grace* from the standard Greek greeting and *peace* from the standard Hebrew greeting, he reminded his readers—who were both Gentile and Jewish—about the inclusiveness of the gospel.

Remember how the gospel came to the Macedonian-city-turned-Roman-colony of Philippi? Two Jewish Roman citizens (Paul and Silas) and the son of a Gentile father (Timothy) arrived in obedience to a vision. And after that trip the newly planted church included the household of a female Jewish proselyte from Asia (Lydia) and that of a Roman official.

Now, recall that the father of the Jewish people was Abraham. And his descendents were fond of identifying with him, too. Remember when Jesus healed the man born blind (John 8)? The Jewish leaders said, basically, "We're *from our father, Abraham*, but we don't know where this Jesus guy is from." So when writing to the church in Philippi, Paul refers to the common parentage that unites Jews and Greeks: The *heavenly Father*, God, and the "the Lord Jesus Christ." And that little detail tells us that *the gospel has enormous social and racial ramifications.*

"Paul knew that many in his congregations were torn by factional strife," writes InterVarsity Press editor, Al Hsu, in *Christianity Today*. "But he didn't say, 'Grace to you Gentiles, and shalom to you Jews.' Grace is not just for Greeks, and peace is not just for Jew. . . So Paul said, 'Grace and peace to you.' Paul addressed Gentile and Jewish believers *together*, as members of one body. He wrote in continuity with their cultural and ethnic backgrounds, yet pointed to a new, countercultural reality. He combined a Greek greeting with a Hebrew greeting to create a distinctively *Christian* greeting."

It's a little like writing "Aloha, y'all!" to a group of Texans and Hawaiians.

Within the church there's no room for bigotry or nationalism or snobbish class divisions. The Cross is the great equalizer. As an African-American pastor told me, "God is not color-blind, as some say. He sees the color—He *made* it. He just doesn't think it *matters*."

How do you treat fellow believers? Do you celebrate racial and cultural diversity within the church? Can you truly say to all who are in Christ, to people of all nations and nationalities, "*Charis* and *shalom* to you through God *our* Father and the Lord Jesus Christ"?

**Pray:** *Thank You, heavenly Father, for adopting me into Your family. Thank You for creating me and opening my heart to receive the good news about Your Son. Break down walls of prejudice in my heart—*

*known and unknown to me—and replace the hardness with Your Spirit's love. Unify Your church, both locally and universally, and please use me as Your slave to do so. Help me to build bridges with my brothers and sisters in Christ that we might demonstrate by our oneness the power of the resurrection. Unite Your children and use us to spread the gospel to the ends of the earth. We ask these things for Your glory and our good through the name of Your Son, Jesus Christ, Amen.*

**Memorize:** "Grace and peace to you from God our Father and the Lord Jesus Christ!" (Phil. 1:1).

# WEEK TWO

*Partnership in the Gospel: Philippians 1:3–30*

Many people say that the theme of the Book of Philippians is joy. And "joy" is certainly a recurring word in Paul's letter. We find it in six different verses. Yet if we think about it, joy is actually a by-product of something else. Paul didn't encourage his readers to pursue joy (though he did tell them to "rejoice"). He didn't even tell them *how* to live the joy-filled life. Rather, for Paul priority one was to spread the good news about Jesus Christ and train people in the faith. And because the Philippians had shared continuously in that priority, Paul rejoiced. So he began, "I thank my God every time I remember you. In all my prayers for all of you, I always pray with joy." Why? "Because of your partnership in the gospel from the first day until now, being confident of this, that he who began a good work in you will carry it on to completion until the day of Christ Jesus. It is right for me to feel this way about all of you, since I have you in my heart; for whether I

41

am in chains or defending and confirming the gospel, all of you share in God's grace with me."

Paul's joy came from seeing their choice to put the gospel first. Notice the many times in the Book of Philippians Paul focused on the gospel:

**1:4–5** I always pray with joy . . . because of your **participation in the gospel** from the first day until now.

**1:7** . . . both in my imprisonment and in the **defense and confirmation of the gospel** all of you became partners in God's grace together with me.

**1:12–14** I want you to know, brothers and sisters, that my situation has actually turned out **to advance the gospel**: The whole imperial guard and everyone else knows that I am in prison for the sake of Christ, and most of the brothers and sisters, having confidence in the Lord because of my imprisonment, now more than ever **dare to speak the word fearlessly.**

**1:18** What is the result? Only that in every way, whether in pretense or in truth, **Christ is being proclaimed**, and in this I rejoice.

**1:27** Only conduct yourselves in a manner **worthy of the gospel** of Christ so that—whether I come and see you or whether I remain absent—I should hear that you are standing firm in one spirit, with one mind, by **contending side by side for the faith of the gospel** . . .

**2:22** But you know his qualifications, that like a son working with his father, he served with me in **advancing the gospel**.

**4:3** Yes, I say also to you, true companion, help them. They have struggled together in the **gospel ministry** along with me . . .

**4:15** And as you Philippians know, at the beginning of my **gospel ministry**, when I left Macedonia, no church shared with me in this matter of giving and receiving except you alone.

It's true that joy as a theme arises many times in this book. But we might more specifically say the overall theme of the book is *joy in response to the furtherance of the gospel*. Just about everything Paul did and thought came back to the priority of knowing Christ and making him known, even if doing so meant enduring hardship.

What is *your* top priority?

1. *Pray for insight. Then read Philippians 1:3-8, which will be the focus of today's time in the Word:*

> **1:3** I thank my God every time I remember you. **1:4** I always pray with joy in my every prayer for all of you **1:5** because of your participation in the gospel from the first day until now. **1:6** For I am sure of this very thing, that the one who began a good work in you will perfect it until the day of Christ Jesus. **1:7** For it is right for me to think this about all of you, because I have you in my heart, since both in my imprisonment and in the defense and confirmation of the gospel all of you became partners in God's grace together with me. **1:8** For God is my witness that I long for all of you with the affection of Christ Jesus.

**"I thank my God"** (1:3)—Notice how Paul tucked in the word "my" when speaking of God. While first-century letters often began with thanksgiving to God, they didn't usually include such personalized statements.

Now, in contemporary English, we use shorter sentences than Paul did. So our translators separate the ideas, but the Greek has one key verb for verses 3–6. Paul wrote the word for "I thank," with the additional phrases subordinate to it:

> I thank my God in all my remembrance of you, always offering prayer with joy in my every prayer for you all, in view of your participation in the gospel from the first day until now, being confident of this very thing, that He who began a good work in you will perfect it until the day of Christ Jesus.

2. According to verse 4, in what manner does Paul offer his prayers?

---

**"I always pray . . . in my every prayer for you all"** (1:4). Notice the constancy in "always" and "every." Whenever Paul prayed for the church in Philippi, he did so with joy, both because he had affection for them and because of their ongoing financial support of his ministry.

We should not assume from the wording here that Paul remembered them randomly, praying for them only when they came to mind.

Because of his Jewish background, he likely had set times for prayer. If you've read Luke's Gospel, you may recall that the day Peter and John healed a lame man, they were going to the temple, as was their custom "at the hour of prayer"—or 3:00 PM (Acts 3:1). During the time when Paul lived, observant Jews stopped to pray at these times:

- early in the morning, in connection with the morning sacrifice
- at 3:00 PM in connection with the evening sacrifice
- at sunset

Some Christian denominations continue to observe set times for prayer throughout the day and night (called "the canonical offices" or the "daily offices"). We don't know for sure that Paul prayed according to such a schedule. But we do know he was grateful for his friends and their support and probably thought of them at least every time he put food in his mouth—sustenance made possible by *them*.

3. What does Paul cite as the cause of his joy (1:5)?

_____

_____

_____

**"Participation"** (1:5)—The word translated "participation" is the Greek word *koinonia*, or fellowship. So Paul prayed with joy because of their "fellowship in the gospel." But he wasn't talking about the kind of "fellowship" in which people have coffee and mingle, nor was he speaking of his communication with or association with them. He was actually not even talking about a more spiritual "fellowship" that involves gathering in Jesus' name. Instead, he was referring to the Philippians' financial expressions of partnership—Lydia's hospitality, sending Epaphroditus to minister to his needs, and monetary gifts—given so Paul can survive and focus on spreading the gospel. Later he will tell his readers that he rejoices not because he benefits from the money they've sent, which he does, but rather in the reward they'll receive for their sacrifice (4:17). He has an eternal perspective.

**"In the gospel"** (1:5)—The tangible partnership the Philippians forged with Paul was focused on the gospel, which means "good news."

The good news Paul spread throughout the inhabited world (at great personal cost) was that Christ died for sins according to the Scripture; He was buried; then He rose on the third day—again, according to scripture. And Paul's message included an emphasis on the ramifications of these great events. Though all have sinned and continue to fall short of God's glory, God laid on his only Son the penalty for sin. As the perfect sacrifice, Jesus Christ was the only one worthy to stand in humanity's place. And while Jesus took the punishment for the sins of the world, the Father credits the Son's righteousness to the account of everyone who believes. Eternal life begins not in heaven, a place. Rather, it begins as reconciliation with God through Christ. It begins when someone trusts in Jesus' finished work and is joined to the family of God.

Have you humbled yourself and believed in Jesus Christ for the forgiveness of your sins? If not, stop and do so right now by talking to God and telling him so.

4. List ways you already "participate" in the gospel.

_____

_____

_____

5. What are some additional ways you can have a part in making the good news a priority?

_____

_____

_____

6. Has anyone ever given to you in a way that made it possible for you to minister in Jesus' name? If so, how?

_____

_____

_____

7. Paul gave thanks for his readers' participation in the gospel "from the first day until now." Think about the first converts in Philippi. Who was present on that "first day" by the river? (If you need a refresher, read again the story you read last week from Acts.)

_____

_____

_____

8. In what ways had Paul benefited from the Philippians' "partnership in the gospel," beginning with that day through the present?

_____

_____

_____

**"The one who began a good work in you will perfect it until the day of Christ Jesus"** (1:6)—Interpreters generally see two options for what Paul meant by "good work" here. One possibility is "sanctification" or "holiness." That is, perhaps Paul was expressing confidence that his readers would continue to grow in conformity to Christ. Just one difficulty—Paul was not talking here about such transformation, important as that is.

The second option seems to fit the context better —that is, the good work relates to the same subject that Paul was already addressing—the Philippians' partnership in the gospel. This makes sense because the dominant theme in the Book of Philippians is that very partnership. The Knox translation captures this idea behind Phil. 1:6, where the gift is more primary: "Nor am I less confident, that he who has inspired this generosity in you will bring it to perfection, ready for the day when Jesus Christ comes."

Sometimes people cite Phil. 1:6 as a promise that God is honor-bound to do a transformative work in the heart of every person who trusts in Christ, and that anyone who truly believes in Christ will never fall away. While the Holy Spirit does transformative work, Paul makes no such promise here relating to all believers. Note the basis for Paul's above statement:

> "For it is right for me to think this about all of you, **because** I have you in my heart, since both in my imprisonment and in the defense and confirmation of the gospel all of **you became partners** in God's grace together with me (1:7).

He doesn't say "it's right for me to think this because that's what the Spirit always does." Rather, he bases his conclusion on a different kind of evidence.

9. On what does Paul base his assurance of his readers' continuing "good work" (1:7)?

_____

_____

_____

_____

10. Does your life show such a strong commitment to spreading the good news about Christ that Paul, if he knew you, could say the same for you? Why or why not?

_____

_____

_____

**"Because I have you in my heart"** (1:7)—The structure of this sentence makes it difficult to know if we should translate it "because you have me in your heart" or as the NET Bible translated it, "because

I have you in my heart." It could be argued well either way. But we resort to word order and context to tell us. Either Paul is expressing how dear they are to him for their kindness or he's saying it's logical for him to appreciate them because their actions have shown how much they value him.

**"My defense and confirmation of the gospel"** (1:7)—Paul may be referring to his trial before Caesar. But this could also include his broader gospel ministry, which the Philippians had supported consistently.

**"You are partners in God's grace"** (1:7)—Grace is unmerited favor. It's getting what we don't deserve—not to be confused with mercy, which is *not* getting what we *do* deserve. Let's say you owe someone $2 million. Mercy wipes out the debt and takes it to a zero balance. Whew! Then grace comes along and adds a $2 million credit.

When it comes to Christ, God's mercy says we don't have to bear the penalty for our own sin any more—the debt is wiped away. But grace goes on to say the balance sheet actually shows a huge credit. All who trust Christ, by God's grace, receive an enormous deposit—Jesus' righteousness credited to our account on the balance sheet! So when God views the Christian believer, He sees Christ's holiness, not because we are perfect, but because God's judicial system is so gracious. And that gift on our account of Christ's righteousness is grace. We have enormous favor with God and we've done nothing to earn it.

Paul considered the Philippians his partners in God's grace. Paul's reference to their partnership was more than a statement of their "family" bond in Christ. Rather, their financial gift made it possible for him to spread the news to Gentiles who had never heard about God's grace.

11. With whom can you share about grace? List and pray for people you know who have never received God's gift of eternal life. Ask God for opportunities to tell of Jesus' love.

_____

_____

_____

_____

12. Pray that God will show you ways He wants you to sacrifice financially for the furtherance of the gospel. Write ideas below that come to mind.

_____

_____

_____

_____

_____

_____

_____

_____

> *For a cultural history of Macedonia focusing on the reign of Philip II and his son, Alexander the Great, check out the DVD* **Macedonia: The Land of a God** *(2004). Archeologist Dimitri Pandermalis, who directed the excavation of Mt. Olympus at Dion, serves as host and visits museums and archeological sites in the ancient kingdom. The program journeys through time in the civilization centers Aina, Aiges, Dion, Pella, Amphipolis, Philippi and Thessaloniki (Thessalonica).*

**"I long for all of you with the affection of Christ Jesus"** (1:8)—Sarah Sumner, author of *Men and Women in the Church*, writes, "It is difficult for people, especially in American Anglo culture, to accept that love does not have to be sexual . . . There is such a thing as 'the affection of Christ Jesus' (Phil. 1:8). I believe he touched people tenderly and bonded with them personally without crossing sexual boundaries. Paul was so affectionate to the Thessalonian Christians that he described himself to them as having been a gentle 'nursing mother' (1 Thess. 2:7). Likewise, he was so emotionally connected to the believers in Ephesus that when God called him to leave, the Ephesian elders 'wept aloud' and 'embraced' and 'repeatedly kissed him' (Acts 20:37)."[2]

13. List the names of some people for whom you have a holy love because of a shared commitment to Christ.

---

[2] Sarah Sumner. *Men and Women in the Church: Building Consensus on Christian Leadership*. Downers Grove, Illinois: InterVarsity Press, 2003, p. 111–112.

_____

_____

_____

14. What are some ways we can express holy love without sexualizing or romanticizing our affection?

_____

_____

_____

## TUESDAY: "THAT GOD WILL GET ME OUT OF HERE" AND OTHER PRAYER REQUESTS PAUL DIDN'T MAKE

1. Ask the Lord by His Spirit to give you insight into the text. Then read Philippians 1:9–11.

> **Philippians 1:9** And I pray this, that your love may abound even more and more in knowledge and every kind of insight **1:10** so that you can decide what is best, and thus be sincere and blameless for the day of Christ, **1:11** filled with the fruit of righteousness that comes through Jesus Christ to the glory and praise of God.

The disciples asked Jesus to teach them to pray. What a great request! How should we talk to God? Jesus gave us a model. And Paul gave us another one. Notice his priority in prayer. It was not "pray that I'll get out of prison" or "that God will heal my body" (many believe Paul had eye problems) or "ask the Lord to give me enough food." That's not to say he would have been wrong to ask for such things. (We know from Philippians 1:19 that he assumed they were praying for his deliverance.) Yet notice what Paul said he talked to God about.

1. For what one key thing did Paul make request (1:9)?

_____

_____

2. In what two ways did he want his readers' love to abound (1:9)?

_____

_____

3. Why did he want this—what was the goal (1:10)?

_____

_____

_____

4. Write out your own prayer for yourself following Paul's model.

_____

_____

_____

"**Be sincere**" (1:10)—The word translated here as *sincere* could also be translated *spotless*, and it has the idea of moral excellence or purity. No hypocrisy. No mixed motives. No duplicity.

"**Blameless**" (1:10)—To be without blame is to avoid either stumbling or causing another to stumble in the faith. Usually Paul used it to refer to the latter.

5. Describe what Paul wanted his readers' sincerity and blamelessness to look like (1:11).

_____

_____

Clearly Paul was focused on his readers' spiritual needs, making no mention of his own trying circumstances. For Paul spiritual concerns far outweigh physical ones. And we need this reminder ourselves.

My theologian friend Eva read a book titled *The Body Project* by Joan Jacobs Brumberg. The author noted that what makes a girl valuable in her own eyes has changed dramatically in the past two hundred years. It has shifted from an internal evaluation of her character and personality to an external evaluation of nearly every feature of her body. Brumberg writes, "When girls in the nineteenth century thought about ways to improve themselves, they almost always focused on their internal character and how it was reflected in outward behavior." Nearly the opposite is true now as "girls today are concerned with the shape and appearance of their bodies as a primary expression of their individual identity."

Girls aren't the only ones. Most men and women seem more focused on improving their tummies and teeth than on internal issues. Consider that between 1997 and 2007, elective cosmetic surgical procedures for women in America increased 142 percent, while nonsurgical procedures increased 743 percent. During the same period, surgical procedures for men increased 3 percent while nonsurgical procedures increased 886 percent.

Paul's first priority was spiritual needs. Jesus, in the Lord's Prayer, had the same emphasis. Still, He included "give us this day our daily bread." Making physical beauty a priority doesn't even show up on the "radar" of either Jesus or Paul. That doesn't mean shabbiness should rule the day, but it does mean we need to evaluate what externals we value, the degree to which we value them, and why.

6. What keeps you from having priorities that are more in line with what Paul expressed (and what God desires for you)?

_____

_____

_____

7. Notice Paul's desire that the Philippians be sincere and blameless "for the day of Christ." Also note Paul's references to such a day in

the New Testament. Most of the occurrences of Paul's phrase "that day" are in Philippians:

> **NIV Romans 2:16** This will take place **on the day** when God will judge men's secrets through Jesus Christ, as my gospel declares.

> **NIV 1 Corinthians 1:8** He will keep you strong to the end, so that you will be blameless **on the day** of our Lord Jesus Christ.

> **NIV Philippians 1:6** being confident of this, that he who began a good work in you will carry it on to completion until **the day of Christ Jesus.**

> **NIV Philippians 1:10** so that you may be able to discern what is best and may be pure and blameless **until the day of Christ,**

> **NIV Philippians 2:16** as you hold out the word of life— in order that I may boast **on the day of Christ** that I did not run or labor for nothing.

Putting these references together, what sort of day did Paul seem to have in view?

8. Why will character issues matter on that day?

_____

_____

_____

9. What is the source of the believer's righteousness (1:11)? What do you think that means?

_____

_____

_____

10. What is the ultimate goal of the abounding, insightful, wise, sincere, blameless righteousness-filled, Christ-given love that Paul envisions (1:11)?

_____

_____

_____

Paul's prayer gives insight into what should be the main focus of every church and ministry. How should we evaluate success? Not by numbers. Not by huge buildings. Not by how many best-selling books our pastors have published. Nor by how many fellowship groups we have. Or how beautiful and well dressed our people are. Or the busyness of our calendars. It's by how well we show mature, Christ-enabled love.

11. Pray through Paul's prayer, asking these things for yourself.

12. Do so again, asking these things for your family and your church, as well as other believers you know.

13. What do you want out of life? Spend some time writing your goals and desires.

_____

_____

_____

14. How do your values, goals, and desires line up with Paul's desires for the church at Philippi? Do you need to alter (altar?) them?

_____

_____

_____

_____

1. Pray for the Holy Spirit to make God's Word clear to you. Then read today's segment, which is Philippians 1:12–21.

> **1:12** I want you to know, brothers and sisters, that my situation has actually turned out to advance the gospel: **1:13** The whole imperial guard and everyone else knows that I am in prison for the sake of Christ, **1:14** and most of the brothers and sisters, having confidence in the Lord because of my imprisonment, now more than ever dare to speak the word fearlessly.
>
> **1:15** Some, to be sure, are preaching Christ from envy and rivalry, but others from goodwill. **1:16** The latter do so from love because they know that I am placed here for the defense of the gospel. **1:17** The former proclaim Christ from selfish ambition, not sincerely, because they think they can cause trouble for me in my imprisonment.
>
> **1:18** What is the result? Only that in every way, whether in pretense or in truth, Christ is being proclaimed, and in this I rejoice. Yes, and I will continue to rejoice, **1:19** for I know that this will turn out for my deliverance through your prayers and the help of the Spirit of Jesus Christ. **1:20** My confident hope is that I will in no way be ashamed but that with complete boldness, even now as always, Christ will be exalted in my body, whether I live or die. **1:21** For to me, living is Christ and dying is gain.

Paul began his letter by assuring his readers that he was okay. Conscious of their concern for him—especially since he was sending back their helper, Epaphroditus—he set his readers at ease. And he also described how God had used his difficulties for good.

2. List all the good things Paul said happened as a result of his imprisonment.

---

---

---

3. Recount a difficult circumstance in your own life and list some ways God has used it for His glory.

_____

_____

_____

Consider the words of Ryan, who left the business world to enter the ministry:

*Is there a parade today?* I looked out the window with a bit of confusion as paper fluttered down from the sky. Working on the twentieth floor of an office building in downtown New York City, I didn't often see objects fall from above. I stood up from my desk, moved into another room to get a better view. . . and gasped in horror at the gaping, burning hole that I saw in the side of the World Trade Center's North Tower.

So began one of the most consequential days of my life. When the Twin Towers fell on September 11, the world changed, and so did I. Up to that point, I was in no rush to do anything significant or meaningful. I had intended to go into ministry since I was a boy, but after graduating college and acquiring a well-paying job in Manhattan, I became comfortable. I was succeeding tremendously at work and I clearly had a future in the company. Overall, I felt secure.

When the second plane flew into the South Tower before my eyes, that sense of security shattered. I remember distinctly wondering what would happen next; *how can we recover from this?* As the Towers toppled, I knew that New York would never be the same, and it wasn't. Little did I know, I would never be the same, either.

The Monday after the Towers fell I returned to work, but a part of me never went back—the part that felt comfortable, the part that felt secure. I looked around the office and saw things with new eyes. The job paid well and it had a future— but it wasn't *my* future. I knew that the Lord had called me to more.

God continues to use a tragedy of mammoth proportions to bring about the furtherance of the gospel in Ryan's life.

Now, we must be clear here. Saying that God can and will use a horrible situation is not at all the same as saying the tragedy itself is good. This is where we sometimes fail to make important distinctions. Those who sought Paul's death did not seek a good thing. They wanted injustice.

What's significant in Paul's letter, though, is that he, the "suffering" person, was the one testifying about how God was bringing good from his difficulty. That same man wrote elsewhere that the observer's job is to "weep with those who weep" (Rom. 12:15). Often we get it backwards, pointing out the good that can come from someone's suffering as they hurt. In doing so we fail to empathize, and we leave *them* weeping, if only on the inside. *We* should be the ones weeping as we identify with their pain. And when they're ready to testify, we should be quiet and listen to what God is doing in their lives.

4. List difficulties you are facing currently and ask God to use your pain for His glory. If you're facing cancer, how can you use your experience to encourage other cancer patients? If you're suffering from insomnia, for whom can you spend the dark, silent hours in prayer? If you're dealing with a rebellious teen, how can you reach out to others in the same situation? If you've had an abortion, where can you tell your story to serve others faced with the same choice? If you're coping with infertility, how can you use that pain as an open door to share Christ with others who hurt?

---

---

---

Paul sums it up: "I want you to know, brothers and sisters, that my situation has actually turned out to advance the gospel" (1:12).

**"Brothers and sisters"** (1:12). The word Paul chose here for "brothers and sisters" is *adelphoi*. You may recognize it as part of the word Phil*adelphia*—the city of brotherly love.

Here's where English differs significantly from Greek—we have separate, very different-sounding nouns for similar concepts where the Greek does not:

English—Siblings          Greek—*Adelphoi*
English—Brothers          Greek—*Adelphoi*
English—Sisters           Greek—*Adelphas*

This makes for a challenge in translation. Sometimes people read translations such as "brothers and sisters" that include the word "sister" and they conclude that the translators have a radical feminist agenda. Yet such is not the case here, nor is it with most translations that use such gender-inclusive language. Consider how quirky it would sound to have Paul writing, "I want you to know, siblings. . ."

> As you study this book of the Bible, if you want to consult a good technical reference that includes insights into the Greek, check out Peter T. O'Brien's Commentary on Philippians.

To translate *adelphoi* as "brothers" would give the idea that Paul had only males in mind. In the past, English-speakers used the word "brothers" to refer to all believers, male and female. Yet the word "brothers" in the past couple of decades has taken on the increasingly limited meaning of male siblings. To capture the apostle's intent, the NET translators chose to include the phrase "and sisters." Paul was writing to the entire church. Besides, in mentioning the Philippians' support "from the first day," he probably had Lydia (the first Philippian convert) and her hospitality in mind.

5. Paul considered fellow believers to be his family. How do or should sibling relationships different from friendship relationships? From romantic relationships?

_____

_____

_____

"**Whole imperial guard**" (1:13)—Other translations say "palace" guard. This likely refers to the praetorian guard, made up of Roman soldiers. Remember, Paul resided in his own rented quarters (Acts 28:30), but soldiers guarded him 24/7. In fact soldiers usually kept prisoners chained to them at the wrist. But that was no problem for Paul. It just meant he had a rotating captive audience! So in a day when people had no TV cameras, radios, internet, or newspapers for announcing news, Paul rejoiced that his story was being told one person at a time until the entire palace guard heard the gospel.

"**And to all the rest**" (1:13)—Paul continued with his list of those who had heard about Christ because of his arrest and imprisonment. In saying "all the rest," he probably meant that "the rest" of the palace personnel (in addition to the entire guard) had heard the gospel because of his circumstances. Rome's most influential people, her up-and-coming leaders, would have resided in the governor's palace. Imagine the opportunity! Paul's sovereign, wise Lord took his servant to a low place so that those in high places could hear and get the word out. How ironic that the ones who sought to silence Paul through imprisonment ended up providing a great platform from which the apostle could proclaim the good news.

Phlippi Today.
Taken from the Acropolis, this photo shows the location of the forum in the foreground and the market in the background.

Paul went on to write another benefit from his difficulties: "And most of the brothers and sisters, having confidence in the Lord because of my imprisonment, now more than ever dare to speak the word fearlessly" (1:14).

**"Having confidence in the Lord because of my imprisonment"** (1:14)—Theodoret, bishop of Cyrrhus, Syria, in the fifth century, wrote this interpretation of Philippians 1:14 in his *Epistle to the Philippians*: "My chains . . . have themselves become the source of courage to the others. They can easily see that I bear adversity with joy. So they come to preach the divine gospel fearlessly."

Have you ever felt empowered by another's courage? Consider my friend Celestin Musekura, who lost six family members following the genocide in Rwanda. Today with his wife he has a Christian reconciliation ministry in Africa. Once when I was eating lunch with them, he mentioned that upon being invited to minister in neighboring Sudan, he prepared himself by lifting weights because he knew if he was captured and imprisoned, his captors would beat his back a set number of times. And he wanted to be well prepared.

My jaw nearly dropped when he mentioned this, as if "prepare for beatings" was just another item on his trip checklist along with "apply for visa" and "get immunizations." He had actually researched the penalty and was preparing himself to face it.

Such people challenge our comfortable self-focused faith, don't they? So often we want our Christianity to bring us comfort, to bless us, to make people respect us for our good works. But Paul, like Celestin after him, was a status-quo-challenging person. Because he spoke boldly, got arrested, and was sharing the gospel with his guards, other believers who heard about Paul's circumstances grew bolder in their own witness. The result? Paul said, "They dare to speak the word fearlessly" (1:14).

Yet, not everyone who spoke of Paul's situation did so out of respect, as he explained:

**1:15** Some, to be sure, are preaching Christ from envy and rivalry, but others from goodwill. **1:16** The latter do so from love because they know that I am placed here for the defense of the gospel. **1:17** The former proclaim Christ from selfish ambition, not sincerely, because they think they can cause trouble for me in my imprisonment.

Imagine the conversation:

"Did you hear they threw Paul in prison? He sure had it coming."

"No! What happened?"

"Let me tell you. . ."

Note what Paul wrote:

**1:18** What is the result? Only that in every way, whether in pretense or in truth, Christ is being proclaimed, and in this I rejoice. Yes, and I will continue to rejoice, **1:19** for I know that this will turn out for my deliverance through your prayers and the help of the Spirit of Jesus Christ. **1:20** My confident hope is that I will in no way be ashamed but that with complete boldness, even now as always, Christ will be exalted in my body, whether I live or die. **1:21** For to me, living is Christ and dying is gain.

6. Paul described two kinds of people who were "gossiping the gospel." What motivated them, according to 1:15?

_____

_____

_____

7. What particularly motivated the second group (1:16)?

_____

_____

_____

8. What motivated the first group (1:17)?

_____

_____

_____

9. What was the end result of all this talk, whether good or slanderous (1:18)?

_____

_____

_____

_____

10. What was Paul's response, current and anticipated (1:18)?

_____

_____

_____

_____

11. What does Paul's response tell you about his top priority?

_____

_____

_____

12. List circumstances Paul was willing to endure cheerfully for the spread of the good news of Christ, according to what you've read so far.

_____

_____

_____

_____

13. What do you think Paul meant by "deliverance" (1:19; see also v. 20)?

_____

_____

_____

_____

14. Why did he expect such an outcome (1:19)?

_____

_____

_____

_____

We might expect Paul to write "my confident hope is that I'll be *so* out of here. And soon." Yet he was more concerned that he might lack boldness than he was about dying. Clearly He had offered his body as a living sacrifice to God (Romans 12:1). And that meant he was willing to face martyrdom, if necessary. He wanted whatever would bring God the most glory.

> **1:20** My confident hope is that I will in no way be ashamed but that with complete boldness, even now as always, Christ will be exalted in my body, whether I live or die. **1:21** For to me, living is Christ and dying is gain.

**"Living is Christ"** (1:20)—For Paul to continue living was Christ, so he used the present tense to emphasize ongoing action.

**"Dying is gain"** (1:20)—For Paul to die was gain, but death had a sense of finality, so he used a different tense—one that emphasized finality. This provided further contrast here between the two poles of life and death.

15. How might God have been exalted in Paul's body if he died? If he lived?

_____

_____

_____

16. How did Paul view life? Death? (1:21).

_____

_____

_____

No matter what happened, they couldn't keep Paul down! Bad circumstances? "Hey, the trials are leading to the furtherance of the gospel!" Imprisonment? "Wow, everybody's hearing about me and why I'm here—and in the process they learn about Christ!" The prospect of martyrdom? "Well, look at it this way—I will be with Christ when I die, right? So that's gain!"

It was all good.

Paul saw God bringing good out of all possible contingencies. Nothing could stop Paul—not life, nor death, nor imprisonment or people preaching the gospel from selfish motives. He believed, as he wrote elsewhere to the Romans, that "God is able to work all things for good to those who love Him and are called according to His purpose" (Romans 8:28). No matter what happened, Paul's only concern seemed to be that he might lack boldness. In terms of his circumstances, he saw the hand of his all-powerful, loving Lord behind everything, leading to ultimate victory.

And this must be our hope, too. No matter what happens, God is in control. God is victor. Our story may stink now, but for those who love Him and are called according to His purpose, long-term it all ends well.

It's all good.

In yesterday's passage, Paul ended with, "For to me, living is Christ and dying is gain." A more familiar translation is, "For me to live is Christ, to die is gain" (Phil 1:21). Keep this in mind as you read what follows in his train of thought.

1. Pray for the Holy Spirit to guide your understanding. Then read today's segment,

> **1:22** Now if I am to go on living in the body, this will mean productive work for me, yet I don't know which I prefer: **1:23** I feel torn between the two, because I have a desire to depart and be with Christ, which is better by far, **1:24** but it is more vital for your sake that I remain in the body. **1:25** And since I am sure of this, I know that I will remain and continue with all of you for the sake of your progress and joy in the faith, **1:26** so that what you can be proud of may increase because of me in Christ Jesus, when I come back to you (Phil. 1:22-26).

Paul explained his "it's all good" mentality by contrasting his only options: living in his mortal body or dying.

2. What were the benefits if Paul continued "living in the body" (1:22, 24)?

_____

_____

_____

Notice that when Paul referred to "earthly life" he didn't just say "living." Whether he was alive in the body or alive in the "afterlife" with Christ, he was living. So he qualified the kind of living he meant: "in the body."

**"I feel torn"** (1:23)—The phrase here is present and passive (rather than Paul acting, it was "done unto" him)—that is, it carries the idea that "continually I am being torn."

3. Why did Paul say he felt torn between the two options—living in the flesh or dying (1:23)?

_____

_____

_____

**"Depart and be with Christ"** (1:23)—Paul's words here tell us several things about the afterlife. First, for the believer death means being with Christ. Second, it suggests there's no intermediate time like "soul sleep" between physically dying and being with Christ. Also, note Paul didn't say "I'll go to heaven," which would emphasize the place, but rather "depart and be with Christ," which emphasized the person, the presence of Christ Himself.

4. Paul ranked his readers' needs over his own personal advantage. What did he decide was the better option in the short term? Why (1:25–26)?

_____

_____

_____

5. Do you want to continue living in your fleshly body, or would you rather die? Why? What's keeping you here?

_____

_____

_____

**"What you can be proud of"** (1:26)—This phrase is rendered in other translations as "that your boast may abound." "Proud" here is not arrogance, but what one celebrates, applauds and exults in. Think of how you feel when an Olympian from your country wins big! You watch the gold medal being placed around his or her neck and you swell with pride as you hear the national anthem. Paul wants his readers to value, to aspire to, or celebrate being established in the faith.

"**May increase**" (1:26)—Or abound or overflow. Rather than preferring death, Paul wanted to return to Philippi so he could continue to teach sound doctrine and his listeners could abound or increase in that which made them proud in the best sense—their growth in Christ.

In conclusion, Paul said he believed God would spare his life for **their** benefit.

6. Why do you think God created you to exist?

_____

_____

_____

7. How are others benefiting from your life?

_____

_____

_____

8. Spend time praying about your life purpose. Ask God to help you to line up your reason for existence with spiritual priorities so that for you "living is Christ."

_____

_____

_____

1. Pray for the Holy Spirit to guide your understanding. Then read today's segment, Philippians 1:27–30.

> **1:27** Only conduct yourselves in a manner worthy of the gospel of Christ so that—whether I come and see you or whether I remain absent—I should hear that you are standing firm in one spirit, with one mind, by contending side by side for the faith of the gospel, **1:28** and by not being intimidated in any way by your opponents. This is a sign of their destruction, but of your salvation—a sign which is from God. **1:29** For it has been granted to you not only to believe in Christ but also to suffer for him, **1:30** since you are encountering the same conflict that you saw me face and now hear that I am facing.

It's easier to see Paul's main focus in this section if we're English teachers considering the structure. In any language writers place their words in a certain order for emphasis. You may not notice it much, but in English we tend to put the word we want to emphasize at the end. Consider the difference between these two sentences:

> Tomorrow I'm going.
> I'm going tomorrow.

In Greek, the word that *begins* a sentence is often the most emphatic. And in Philippians 1:27, Paul begins with the word "only"—as in, "above all." Let's look at a rough diagram of his words so we can see what else he wants to emphasize.

> Only conduct yourselves worthily
> So whether A or B happens, I will hear
> You're standing firm
> In one spirit
> With one mind
> By contending side by side
> For the faith
> Of the gospel
>
> [And I will hear]
> You're not being intimidated
> In any way by your opponents. . .

By looking at it this way, we can see how Paul's imperative to "only conduct yourselves in a manner worthy" stands out as the main idea. He wanted the Philippians to live lives consistent with the gospel or suitable to it.

**"Conduct yourselves"** (1:27)—We translate these two words in English from one word in Greek, and it's a word with strong political nuances. Paul's readers would have recognized that it carried the idea of living as *citizens*. That is, "discharge your obligations as citizens in a way that's gospel-worthy." Paul wanted the citizenship-conscious people of Philippi to obtain their identity as citizens from their connection to the heavenly country to which they belonged, conducting themselves as good representatives of *that* kingdom. They needed to order their privileges and responsibilities according to the gospel.

Remember Philippi's identity—it was a Roman colony in a Greek world. The people of Philippi wore their Roman citizenship like a badge. You'll recall how the city magistrates in Philippi stopped mistreating Paul once they discovered he possessed citizenship rights. In his writings, Paul challenged the Philippians to identify more closely with their heavenly country. That meant acting differently from the culture around them. They needed to live consistently with *who* they were more than *where* they were.

Sometimes believers in North America make political decisions based on party affiliations over their faith in Christ and His Word. They may sacrifice unity because they disagree with someone who belongs to a political party, even questioning how someone can be a Christian and vote the way they do.

Some churches include the pledge of allegiance to the U.S. flag in their July 4 services. (Imagine sitting there as a Christ-follower from France or Canada or Australia.) While we should be good earthly citizens, we must never allow our national citizenship or affiliation with a political party to take precedence over our identity as heavenly citizens.

2. Why does Paul want his readers to walk worthy of the gospel (1:27)?

_____

_____

_____

3. Paul gives specific descriptions about what worthy living looks like. Write a want-ad for the kind of reputation Paul desires for his readers to have, according to 1:27-28.

**Wanted:**

4. Note Paul's emphasis on unity, oneness, and standing side-by-side (see 1:27 below). Why do you think unity is such an essential ingredient in worthy conduct?

_____

_____

_____

5. Reread Phil. 1:27–30. What terms suggest the presence of conflict and opposition? Do you think Paul considered these the norm or exceptions in the Christian life?

_____

_____

_____

6. Of what two things was the opposition to their faith a sign (1:28)?

_____

_____

_____

7. What (or rather, who) did Paul say was the ultimate source of the "sign," the opposition (1:28)?

_____

_____

_____

**Philippians 1:27** Only conduct yourselves in a manner worthy of the gospel of Christ so that—whether I come and see you or whether I remain absent—I should hear that you are standing firm in one spirit, with one mind, by contending side by side for the faith of the gospel, **1:28** and by not being intimidated in any way by your opponents. This is a sign of their destruction, but of your salvation—a sign which is from God. **1:29** For it has been granted to you not only to believe in Christ but also to suffer for him, **1:30** since you are encountering the same conflict that you saw me face and now hear that I am facing.

_The Voice of the Martyrs is a non-profit organization created to aid persecuted Christians around the world, fulfilling the Great Commission, and educating the world about the ongoing persecution of Christians. Pray for your brothers and sisters enduring persecution worldwide. You can find out more at persecution.com._

**"This is a sign of their destruction, but of your salvation"** (1:28)—Persecution provides tangible evidence of the hatred some have for Christ and the lengths to which they will go to silence those who believe. So in that sense, persecution is a sign to the saints of their opponents' coming destruction on the Day of Judgment. On the other hand, the endurance of a believer in persevering through persecution for the sake of Christ indicates the presence of the Holy Spirit. Have you ever heard of unbelieving prisoners who, rather than complaining or cursing or threatening, spent their first night in jail singing and rejoicing? No. We cannot explain such behavior apart from the Spirit and grace of God. In our own strength, we don't act that way!

8. The word "for" in v. 29 indicates the "why" or "purpose" behind "a sign of God." For what reason did Paul say God "granted" for

Christians to be persecuted (1:29-30)?

_____

_____

_____

**"Granted"** (1:29)—This verb suggests a gift, a free favor or kindness. And what gift was God granting? Paul mentioned two: ". . . not only to believe in Christ *but also to suffer for him.*" We don't generally think of suffering as a gift!

Paul Brand, the renowned hand surgeon coauthored a book with Philip Yancey titled, *Pain: The Gift Nobody Wants.* That title captures the kneejerk reaction most of us have to difficulty. Yet Paul encourages his readers to view persecution as a God-okayed blessing.

Paul's words echo those of our Lord, who told his listeners that they were blessed when persecuted because a) the persecuted are in good company—people ridiculed the prophets, too; and b) the persecuted will receive a great reward in heaven (see Matthew 5).

Now, sometimes we bring difficulties on ourselves and claim we're being persecuted when we're not. I recall some years ago a Christian book store (long since out of business) claimed the City of Dallas was persecuting them. It turned out that their "persecution" was that they received notification that their store violated a city code that limited the number of flags they could fly outside the store. The ordinance allowed two; the store had three—the U.S. flag, the Texas flag, and the Christian flag. But the store spun the story as, "The City is making us take down the Christian flag." That's not persecution.

The kind of persecution Paul had in mind was enduring anything from rolled eyes to the death penalty *because of one's identification with Christ.*

It's significant that in a short book so focused on "the gospel" and on bold proclamation of the good news that Paul would also mention suffering. The two generally go hand in hand.

We should not pursue suffering or seek to be persecuted. But we should seek to proclaim the good news about Christ, unashamed of our identification with Him. Paul assumed that those who did so would face hardship.

9. What do Paul's words suggest about what the Philippians were facing (1:30)?

_____

_____

_____

10. Have you ever faced ridicule or difficulty solely *because you're a Christian*? If not, why not?

_____

_____

_____

11. Spend some time praying for the persecuted church. And pray for your own witness that you will be wise, bold, and courageous, counting it a privilege if God allows you to suffer for identifying yourself with the name of Christ.

_____

_____

_____

## SATURDAY: THAT RADIOACTIVE LITERATURE

**Philippians 1:12, 18** I want you to know, brothers and sisters, that my situation has actually turned out to advance the gospel . . . What is the result? Only that in every way, whether in pretense or in truth, Christ is being proclaimed, and in this I rejoice.

Inauguration Day, 1981. For the first time in history, an actor took the U.S. presidential oath of office. And that same day, after holding them for more than 400 days in captivity, Iran released fifty-two American hostages. Washington was electric. Nobody was worried about terrorists. Streamers flew and crowds cheered.

My young husband, Gary, and I were among the numerous citizens who had poured into our nation's capitol to participate in the festivities and catch a glimpse of the presidential motorcade. We had come with a group of our peers, college students, with the assignment to spend the first hour handing out commemorative brochures that included the gospel.

Several groups didn't receive our free leaflets: the hard-rock rebels who refused them, the folks in fur coats who also turned them down, and the inaccessible dignitaries in roped-off areas requiring special tickets.

Gary and I teamed up with a third person and together we had a box of tracts. But we soon grew weary of lugging it around, so we found a spot near a statue on the Ellipse (the President's Park South across from the White House) and set it down. Then each of us took as many brochures as we could carry in our hands and fanned out to distribute them.

I was the first to return for more. As I approached, I noticed people in uniforms roping off the area. I quickly scooted in to grab the box, but one of them stopped me.

"Where are you going?" he asked.

I pointed to the cardboard. "That's my box. I just need—"

"That's *your* box?" He didn't bother to conceal his alarm. "What's in it?"

*Whoa.* I took a second look at my surroundings. Two SWAT trucks sat parked on the curb. Somebody was getting out a metal detector and the area was roped off. All because of the box.

I meekly held up one of the leaflets and squeaked out, "These."

About that time, my husband arrived and asked what all the commotion was about. A crowd gathered around us to hear what the men were saying.

The guys with metal detectors started in on the box. "There's nothing harmful in there," my husband told the man who was talking to us. "We just set it down for a minute."

"Maybe you didn't put anything harmful in it," he said. "But someone else could come along after you and put a bomb in there."

We stood there, knees shaking. The man kept an eye on his friend scanning our box, but he reassured us with, "I'm sure it was an innocent mistake." Still, he warned us never, ever to set a box down near the White House.

We waited while the SWAT team gingerly opened the box to find . . . only tracts inside. But by the time they finished taking apart their equipment and removing the ropes, the crowd was enormous. Hundreds now surrounded us.

After we got our box back people pressed in and clamored for its contents. Hard rockers said they wanted our "radioactive literature." People in fur coats wanted copies so they could pass them along to friends. And the people in the roped-off area sent a representative to obtain some samples for them. We ran out of supplies in seconds.

God has his ways of getting the gospel out, doesn't he? Sometimes even when people have ulterior motives. And certainly even when His servants make dumb mistakes.

In his book *The God Delusion*, atheist Richard Dawkins says what he opposes about religion, but in the process, ends up giving a clear presentation of the gospel of Christ. He writes, "God incarnated himself as a man, Jesus, in order that he should be tortured and executed in atonement for the hereditary sin of Adam. Ever since Paul expounded this repellent doctrine, Jesus has been worshipped as the redeemer of our sins. Not just the past sin of Adam: future sins as well."

Who would think the gospel of our Lord could be found inside a work promoting atheism?

As Paul said, the important thing is that "Christ is preached. And in this I rejoice and will rejoice (Phil 1:18).

We can't stop God. He can use anything!

**Pray:** *Thank You, Father, that in Your great love for us You sent Your Son. Thank You for those before me who have sacrificed so much—even given their lives—so that the gospel might spread to me and to the rest of the world. Please use me to bring glory to Yourself. And grant me the wisdom to know what sacrifices I can and should make that others might know You. Thank You for the joy that comes in participating in the gospel. Thank you for the peace that comes from Your Holy Spirit. Help me to live in a way that's worthy of all You've done for me. In Jesus' name, Amen.*

**Memorize:** "For to me, living is Christ and dying is gain." (Phil. 1:21)

# WEEK THREE

## *Emptied But Not Less: Philippians 2*

**Scripture:** For it has been granted to you not only to believe in Christ but also to suffer for him. (Phil. 1:29)

Every spring *Christianity Today* magazine announces what they deem the ten top religion stories from the previous year. One year number seven was about the torture and martyrdom of three Christians in eastern Turkey. Some months later, during missions conference week at a Texas seminary, students gained a behind-the-scenes perspective on that story from the school's first-ever student from Turkey.

The student, Yuce Kabakci, told of how three employees of a publishing house that distributes Bibles were murdered in an attack that targeted Turkey's Christian minority. (Turkey is the largest unreached country in the world with a 98% Muslim population.) The three victims, a German and two Turkish citizens, were found with their hands and legs bound. But what's worse, when the attackers heard police entering the building, they slit their victims' throats.

One of those Turkish citizens was Yuce's mentor. Imagine hearing that someone you love has endured that kind of horror for the sake of Christ. (How Jesus must have felt when he learned that his relative, John, had been beheaded!) After describing these events, Yuce left the audience with a challenge: "When you preach the gospel, do not say 'God has a wonderful plan for your life.' Tell people, 'Jesus is worth dying for.'"

When I emailed to ask Yuce if I could tell his story without endangering him, he wrote this:

> I'm so honored to hear that what God has done through me will be declared to others as well. . . I am already dead to the world, and since no one can kill me twice, I don't have any issues like remaining anonymous or anything like that. You can use my full name and full information. Before I came to [seminary], I would (and still do) get some threat emails from some fanatical Muslims. What I usually do is to invite them to my church and promise them that I will be there at the given hour. None of them showed up. If anything that I did, do, or will do is going to glorify God, then the rest is irrelevant.

Often in our Westernized view of the faith we get the idea—and export it—that the Christian life is all peace and joy and love. It's our best life now. Yet when we do so, we have to stop and ask ourselves whether we have any clue what it means to follow the One who was basically kicked out of Nazareth, unwanted in Jerusalem, and nailed to a tree.

When we tell people, "God has a wonderful plan for your life," in the context of only the here and now, we foster a mentality that says, "I'll follow God to get the perks." Even when we utter, "Please grant success to our efforts" we may mean "add to our numbers so we'll look cool" rather than concern for the furtherance of the gospel. We don't want to sacrifice, to persevere. We want even service for Him to bring us comfort in this life rather than waiting for our reward in the next.

Paul's emphasis on the gospel in Philippians reminds us that, like Yuce, we press on not because of possible short-term benefits. We do so because the one we follow, the one who gave His life for us, is worth dying for.

1. Pray for the Holy Spirit to grant you insight and a teachable heart. Then read today's Scripture, Philippians 2:1–4.

> **Phil. 2:1** Therefore, if there is any encouragement in Christ, any comfort provided by love, any fellowship in the Spirit, any affection or mercy, **2:2** complete my joy and be of the same mind, by having the same love, being united in spirit, and having one purpose. **2:3** Instead of being motivated by selfish ambition or vanity, each of you should, in humility, be moved to treat one another as more important than yourself. **2:4** Each of you should be concerned not only about your own interests, but about the interests of others as well.

"**Therefore**" (2:1)—It's been said that if you're reading the Bible and you come upon the word *therefore*, you should "find out what it's there for." I'll add to that: And to find out what it's there for, back up a paragraph and find the main idea that precedes it.

In this case immediately preceding *therefore* was Paul's imperative to "conduct yourselves (citizenwise) in a manner worthy of the gospel." So he used "therefore" as a transition from the imperative to walk worthy to explaining how the Philippians can do so. Yet first he paused to lay a foundation for *why*.

"**If**" (2:1)—Sometimes we use the word "if" to express the possibility of doubt or contingency: "If you want to go with me to the store, we need to leave now." The one who hears it may or may not wish to go.

Yet sometimes we use "if" as almost synonymous with "since." Example: "If I've taught you any manners at all (and I have), would you please chew with your mouth closed?"

Greek has a number of "if" constructions. And the kind Paul chose here carry the latter idea: "If these four things are true—and we know they are—make my joy complete." He was not suggesting doubt in any way. Rather, he was highlighting truths that the Philippians held to be self-evident.

2. In 2:1, Paul listed four basic assumptions, each of which started with "any." What are they?

If there is . . .

any:

_____

_____

any:

_____

_____

any:

_____

_____

any:

_____

_____

Paul went on to persuade his readers on the basis of what they already knew to be true because of Christ's saving work. Let's look at each of these individually.

"**Encouragement in Christ**" (2:1)—Paul probably wasn't talking about interpersonal encouragement that Christians offer each other, wonderful as that is. Rather he was referring to the consolation of the soul brought through Christ Himself and his finished work on the cross.

Some years ago when I was in Minsk, Belarus, some fellow believers and I went to call on a man whose friend felt we could help him. A philosopher, he had studied all the world's major religions except Christianity. And a nagging question tormented his soul: "How can I get rid of my sins?" He had such a sense of God's holiness and his own sinfulness that he knew he never could do enough works to compensate. He told us he hoped we might have an answer.

What a great question!

When we told him the good news about Christ *taking away* sins by bearing them on Himself, this man, through misty eyes, suddenly stopped speaking in Russian and spoke in English. His words: "I love you!"

Sometimes we grow so used to seeing eyes roll at the presentation of the gospel that we forget what wonderful news it is. Our sins are forgiven—gone! What encouragement in Christ!

**"Comfort provided by love"** (2:1)—Great comfort comes from knowing, "Yes, Jesus loves me." The Philippians needed God's consolation as they faced persecution. In their city people worshiped the emperor as god. Because Christ-followers refused to engage in emperor-worship their neighbors accused them of treason. Imagine such an accusation in a city that prides itself in Roman citizenship, a city known for being "Rome in Greece." In the midst of such scorn, it's easy to think, "God must hate me." Yet the opposite is true. What a relief to know the comfort of Christ's love.

**"Fellowship in the Spirit"** (2:1)—Remember how Paul used the word "fellowship" earlier in his letter? He didn't mean coffee-hour fellowship. He meant "participation." The Philippian believers were connected to the Spirit and as such they had "participation in the Spirit."

Sometimes when we need wisdom to make difficult decisions, we say stuff like, "I wish God would fax me an answer" or "I wish God would write 'yes' or 'no' in the clouds." Yet we actually do have One who guides us even more intimately than through a fax or the clouds, One who lives within each person who follows Christ. We are never, ever alone. "I will be with you" is one of our most cherished promises.

**"Affection or mercy"** (2:1)—The word "or" here does not necessarily have the idea of choice as we would use it to ask, "Should I wear the red dress *or* the green dress?" Instead, it may be a figure of speech called a hendiadys (hen-DIE-uh-dis). Think of the expression "sick and tired" as in "I'm sick and tired of seeing your room so messy." The person who makes such a statement is neither ill nor physically exhausted. "Sick and tired," when used as one phrase, expresses the singular idea of being weary. Worn out. If "affection or mercy" is a hendiadys, it has the idea of "heartfelt sympathy." This is how most translators understand it.

Yet in keeping with Paul's three previous ideas, it is also quite possible (and seems more likely to me) that he was referring to both Christ's affection for and His mercy toward Christians. In Greek the same word can be translated "and" or "or." We try to determine which he intends by looking at the context. So think of the tenderest mother, the most doting father, a friend who weeps when you do, and you have several crude pictures of God's infinite affection *and* mercy.

Put these four together—encouragement in Christ, comfort of love, fellowship in the Spirit, and affection and mercy—and you have a great summary of why it's so wonderful to know Christ. Believers have all of these in common. And as one commentator wrote, "The Philippians know God's comfort and salvation in Christ. They have experienced that Christ's love for them has brought in their sufferings and dangers. Theirs is a participation, a common sharing, in the Holy Spirit, and they have been blessed through his gracious ministry to their hearts and lives. When God began his good work in their midst though the preaching of the gospel, they were recipients of his tender mercies and compassion. Since they have been blessed with such riches in a magnificent way, let them hear Christ's exhortation through their beloved apostle."[3]

From the above four benefits that every Christian has, Paul provides a springboard to jump into how he wants his readers to live as a result.

**"Complete my joy"** (2:2)—The word *complete* could also be translated *fulfill*. The phrase suggests that Paul already has some joy. Remember, he's writing a missionary thank-you letter. He already overflows with gratitude for their partnership in the gospel expressed to him through prayers, money, and sending someone to help. Now he wants them to put the icing on the cake. John Chrysostom (A.D. 347–407), the early church father and archbishop of Constantinople, wrote of this verse, "[Paul] does not want this exhortation to appear to be addressed to those who have failed in their duty. So he does not say 'give me joy' but 'complete my joy.' That is as if to say: 'You have already begun to flourish. You have already pursued peace as I wish. Now I long for you to reach the highest levels of maturity in faith.' "[4]

3. The Philippians needed to *have* two things and *be* two things to complete Paul's joy. What were those things (2:2)?

[3] O'Brien, Peter. *New International Greek Testament Commentary: Commentary on Philippians.* (Grand Rapids, MI: Wm. B. Eerdmans Publishing Co., 1991), 176.
[4] HOMILY ON PHILIPPIANS 6.2.1–4. IOEP 5:51.

Being:

_____

_____

Having:

_____

_____

Being:

_____

_____

Having:

_____

_____

4. Notice how Paul repeated words and ideas to emphasize his point. Summarize what Paul wanted more than anything.

_____

_____

_____

As mentioned, the Philippians faced challenges from without and within the church. From outside, they faced persecution. Add to these the challenges that come from within. Paul had already told them how to deal with outsiders. Then he shifted his focus to helping his readers avoid difficulties with each other.

5. Paul contrasted what they should not do and what they should do. What should the Philippians *not* do (2:3)?

_____

_____

_____

6. What do you see as the difference between being ambitious and having selfish ambition?

_____

_____

_____

7. Behind divisions in Christ's Body are people living self-focused lives. And we're all vulnerable. In the words of our Lord, "the spirit is willing but the flesh is weak" (Mark 14:38). What are some ways vanity affects us and those we know?

_____

_____

_____

8. Instead of being consumed by self-focus, what did Paul want the Philippians to do (2:3)?

_____

_____

_____

Gaius Marius Victorinus (c. 300–370), an African by birth, was a Roman grammarian, rhetorician, and philosopher. He also made a marked impression on the church fathers Augustine and Jerome. And in Victorinus's commentary, *Epistle to the Philippians*, he wrote this of Paul's exhortation here: "Many are either prone toward ambitiousness of their own accord or moved toward ambitiousness through others. All these kinds of ambition are to be banished. There is to be no inordinate ambition, whether voluntary or constrained, since both are vicious. Some rush into this ambition through speculation; others are naturally of such temper as to be ambitious. So [Paul] advises: 'do nothing through ambition.' "[5]

9. What are some risks and benefits of treating others as more important than ourselves?

_____

_____

_____

10. How does putting someone else's interests above our own differ from enabling someone's destructive behavior?

_____

_____

_____

11. Paul added an additional contrast. What did he say the Philippians should not be? What should they be, instead (2:4)?

_____

_____

_____

[5] *Epistle to the Philippians* 2.2.5, BT 1972:82–83 [1205C–D].

"One cannot be both a slave to popularity and a true servant of God."[6]—JOHN CRYSOSTOM

12. Share a time when someone put your interests above his or her own and how it affected you.

_____

_____

_____

13. Think of a time when you put someone else's interests above your own. Was it difficult? Why or why not?

_____

_____

_____

Some years ago when my husband and I taught college students at our church, we overheard one of the guys saying, "The Bible tells me I need to consider others' interests as equal with my own."

Though he'd said it with great humility—as if this was a real challenge for him but he was determined to do it—when we told him, "No, it says to consider others' interests *as more important* than your own," he couldn't believe it. We had to show him the passage before he believed us. Putting others first goes against what happens naturally!

14. Think of your relationships with other believers. List three tangible ways that you can, through the enablement of the Spirit, put someone else's interests above your own in the week ahead.

_____

_____

[6] IOEP 5:52.

15. Spend some time in prayer, thanking Christ for what He has done for you and asking God to help you put others first.

_____

_____

_____

## TUESDAY: CHRISTMAS ACCORDING TO PAUL

1. Often Christian marriage conferences focus only on the Bible verses that specifically relate to marriage. Yet any time two sinners join themselves to each other, we should include Philippians 2. Paul has just told his readers that to complete his joy they must humble themselves and think of others first. Now he goes on to present Christ Jesus as the ultimate example of both of these. The Second Person of the Trinity, fully God, demonstrated His humility in "not clinging to equality," but emptying Himself. In doing so He learned to obey, taking on the form of a slave, and dying on a cross. He put others first as He, the sinless One, bore the penalty of sin for humanity when we could not help ourselves. What other human has gone so far to put another first?

_____

_____

_____

2. Read worshipfully the short hymn that comprises the verses for today and tomorrow:

> **2:5** You should have the same attitude toward one another that Christ Jesus had,
>
> **2:6** who though he existed in the form of God
> did not regard equality with God
> as something to be grasped,
> **2:7** but emptied himself
> by taking on the form of a slave,
> by looking like other men,

and by sharing in human nature.
**2:8** He humbled himself,
by becoming obedient to the point of death
—even death on a cross!
**2:9** As a result God exalted him
and gave him the name
that is above every name,
**2:10** so that at the name of Jesus
every knee will bow
—in heaven and on earth and under the earth—
**2:11** and every tongue confess
that Jesus Christ is Lord
to the glory of God the Father.

3. What point was Paul stressing that led him to describe Jesus' humility (v. 5)?

_____

_____

_____

_____

In the 1980s, a *Time* magazine cover story asked "Who was Jesus?" Two decades later, Dan Brown's *The Da Vinci Code* questioned again Jesus' humanity and divinity. Who does the Bible say Jesus is? Human? God? Both? Many have tried to rework His identity, insisting that He walked on ice, not water and that He didn't take on human flesh—that He was only a spirit. Cults say he was a great prophet and nothing more. These and ideas like them are nothing new; they're simply old deceptions repackaged. But they raise important issues. Do we know the fundamentals of our own faith? Who does the Bible say Jesus is and was? Who has the church understood Jesus to be for twenty centuries? What is the ancient faith as handed down to us? Paul takes the opportunity to teach his readers about humility while telling them who Christ is.

**"He existed in the form of God"** (2:6)—The Son of God existed before His own birth. That is why we say of Christ that he was "begotten not created." (Think of the words in "O Come, All Ye

Faithful.") God created you and me from egg and sperm, but "in the beginning" Christ, the Word, "was with God and the Word was God" (see John 1:1). He was and is and is to come.

*Jesus existed in the form of God.* The word "form" in Phil. 2:6 is translated from *morphe* from which we get the word *metamorphosis.* Sometimes in English we use "form" to mean the outward shape of something—as in, "The cake has a round form." Yet that's not how Paul uses it. He is speaking of Christ's essential nature or actual substance rather than only His outward appearance. Paul is saying that in His nature, Jesus was God. Yet He took on the form, or essential nature, of a servant. Keep in mind the point Paul is making here in the broader context—that of the absolute humility of the Son. The Son *was* God, yet He humbled himself.

The nature of Jesus Christ has been the subject of past councils, and orthodox theologians have written volumes on it. Heretics have said Jesus was fully human but not fully God; that He was fully God but not fully human; that he was half-human and half-God; that he had a human body, but a divine mind and spirit; that he had two separate persons—one divine and one human; that he had only one nature, the human absorbed into the divine; and that He is below the Father in a hierarchy. All such ideas are erroneous. The Chalcedonian Council was convened in 451 to articulate orthodox theology, and together the world's top Christian theologians, after searching the scriptures rigorously, wrote the Chalcedonian Creed:

> We, then, following the holy Father, all with one consent, teach men to confess one and the same Son, our Lord Jesus Christ, the same perfect in Godhead and also perfect in manhood; truly God and truly man; of a reasonable/rational soul and body; consubstantial (having the same nature or substance) with the Father according to the Godhead, and consubstantial with us according to the Manhood; in all things like unto us, without sin; begotten before all ages of the Father according to the Godhead, and in these latter days, for us and for our salvation, born of the Virgin Mary, the Mother of God, according to the Manhood; one and the same Christ, Son, Lord, Only-begotten, to be acknowledged in two natures inconfusedly, unchangeably, indivisibly, inseparably; the distinction of the natures being by no means taken away by the union, but rather the property of each nature being preserved,

and concurring in one person and one subsistence, not parted or divided into two persons, but one and the same Son, and only begotten, God, the Word, the Lord Jesus Christ, as the prophets from the beginning have declared concerning him, and the Lord Jesus Christ himself has taught us, and the Creed of the holy Fathers has been handed down to us.

4. What wrong views about Christ's nature have you encountered?

_____

_____

_____

## WEDNESDAY: EMPTIED BUT NOT WORTHLESS

1. Re-read the verses you read yesterday:

**Philippians 2:5** You should have the same attitude toward one another that Christ Jesus had,

**2:6** who though he existed in the form of God
did not regard equality with God
as something to be grasped,
**2:7** but emptied himself
by taking on the form of a slave,
by looking like other men,
and by sharing in human nature.
**2:8** He humbled himself,
by becoming obedient to the point of death
—even death on a cross!
**2:9** As a result God exalted him
and gave him the name
that is above every name,
**2:10** so that at the name of Jesus
every knee will bow
—in heaven and on earth and under the earth—
**2:11** and every tongue confess
that Jesus Christ is Lord
to the glory of God the Father.

**"[He] did not regard equality with God as something to be grasped"** (2:6)—I used to think the word "grasped" here served as a synonym for "comprehended"—as we might say, "I just can't grasp that concept." I wondered how Jesus could possibly be omniscient yet fail to comprehend His equality with the Father!

But the Greek word for "grasped" can mean either "robbery" or "cling to/clutch," depending on the context. Certainly the Son did understand His equality with the Father. And the only one equal to God is God!

So picture the Son as the complete equal next to the Father holding a scepter in His hand. Then picture him voluntarily handing the scepter to the Father, stepping down from the throne to enter time and space, and putting on the clothes of a servant. His actions say that, even though He is equal with the Father, he is not going to cling to that equality; instead He's going to "empty Himself," taking on that low-status form. Imagine the humility involved! We learn elsewhere that for a time, the second Person of the Trinity ranked even lower than the angels (Hebrews 2:9).

2. Which of these two statements best echoes the truth in this verse? Circle one.

a. "Being already below the Father in hierarchy, the Son acted in conformity with His role by submitting when the Father sent him."

b. "Being equal with God in every way, the Son did not consider equality with God something to cling to, but instead placed Himself below the Father, taking on the form of a servant."

Consider what some of the church fathers have written about this verse:

EUSEBIUS OF VERCELLI (283–371): Where there is one equality, neither is prior to the other. Neither is posterior nor subordinate, since there is no distinction in the united equality, which is the fullness of divinity. ON THE TRINITY 3.4, 7.[7]

CHRYSOSTOM (c. 347–400): When someone who has the power to think great thoughts humbles himself, that one is humble. But when his humility comes from impotence, that is not what you would call humility. . . . It is a humility of a greater sort to refrain

[7] CCL 9:32–33.

from "seizing" power, to be "obedient to death." HOMILY ON PHILIPPIANS 7.2.5–8.[8]

AUGUSTINE (354–386): Wherein lies the Son's equality? If you say in greatness, there is no equality of greatness in one who is less eternal. And so with other things. Is He perhaps equal in might but not equal in wisdom? Yet how can there be equality of might in one who is inferior in wisdom? Or is he equal in wisdom but not equal in might? But how can there be equality of virtue in one who is inferior in power? Instead Scripture declares more simply "he thought it not robbery to be equal." Therefore every adversary of truth who is at all subject to apostolic authority must admit that the Son is in some one respect at least the equal of God. Let him choose whichever quality he might wish, but from that it will appear that he is equal in all that is attributed to divinity. ON THE TRINITY 6.5.[9]

**"He emptied himself"** (2:7)—The word translated as emptied is a derivative of the root word *kenosis*. You may have heard of "the doctrine of the kenosis." It refers to the great "emptying of Himself" which Jesus accomplished by actually taking on or adding something—the form of a servant. Note that Paul does not say the Father commanded Him or that the Father emptied Him. Jesus did it of his own free will. And Paul does not say Jesus emptied himself of *something*, such as his deity or even of the rights of deity. Rather, it was him*self* that he emptied. Jesus never gave up being God! The text goes on to describe the way in which He emptied Himself: *by taking on the form of a servant.* "He emptied His glory by veiling it in humanity."[10]

Consider, again, what those who have pondered these thoughts in centuries past have concluded:

ORIGEN (185–232): In "emptying himself," He became a man and was incarnate while remaining truly God. Having become a man, He remained the God that He was. He assumed a body like our own, differing only in that it was born from the Virgin by the Holy Spirit. ON FIRST PRINCIPLES 1, PREFACE 4.[11]

AUGUSTINE: He is said to have "emptied himself" in no other way than by taking the form of a servant, not by losing the form of God.

[8] IOEP 5:62–63.
[9] PL 42:926–27.
[10] Daniel B. Wallace. *Greek Grammar beyond the Basics* (Grand Rapids: Zondervan Publishing House, 1996), 220.
[11] GCS 22:10; from Rufinus's Latin translation.

CONTRA FAUSTUM 3.6.[12]

GREGORY OF ELVIRA (c. 375): We do not believe that He was so emptied that He himself as Spirit became something else. Rather He, having put aside for this time the honor of his majesty, put on a human body. Only by assuming human form could He become the Savior of humanity. Note that when the sun is covered by a cloud its brilliance is suppressed but not darkened. . . So too that man, whom our Lord Jesus Christ put on, being our Savior, which means God and the Son of God, does not lessen but momentarily hides the divinity in him. ON THE FAITH 88–89.[13]

3. "By" what three ways did Jesus empty himself (v. 7)?

_____

_____

_____

4. In what way did Jesus humble himself? (vv. 7–8)?

_____

_____

_____

5. What was the result (vv. 8–11)?

_____

_____

_____

_____

[12] PL 42:218.
[13] CCL 69:244.

6. What future event is described here as the end result of Jesus' humility (vv. 10–11)? List those who will bow the knee and confess Christ in the future.

_____

_____

_____

7. Why do you think Paul chose this extended example to make the point that Christ-followers should put others first?

_____

_____

_____

**"God exalted him . . . so that at the name of Jesus every knee will bow . . . and every tongue confess that Jesus Christ is Lord** (2: 9–11)—Paul was making literary reference (not a direct quote but an allusion) to the Old Testament here to ground his words about Christ in what his readers knew about God. In Isaiah's prophecy the Lord is speaking, and He says this:

> Turn to me so you can be delivered,
> all you who live in the earth's remote regions!
> For I am God, and I have no peer.
> I solemnly make this oath —
> what I say is true and reliable:
> "Surely every knee will bow to me,
> every tongue will solemnly affirm;
> they will say about me,
> 'Yes, the LORD is a powerful deliverer.' " (Isa. 45:22–24)

Paul quoted Isaiah elsewhere when talking about the day we'll stand before God:

> For we will all stand before the judgment seat of God. For it is written, "As I live, says the Lord, every knee will bow to me, and

every tongue will give praise to God." Therefore, each of us will give an account of himself to God (Rom. 14:11).

Paul trusted his readers to make the connection that Christ will fulfill Isaiah's prophecy about Yahweh. Clearly Paul considered Christ to be deity.

**"To the glory of God the Father"** (v. 11)—While on earth, Jesus spoke of His "Father who glorifies Me" (John 8:54). Four chapters later John wrote, "When therefore he had gone out, Jesus said, 'Now is the Son of Man glorified, and God is glorified in Him; if God is glorified in Him, God will also glorify Him in Himself, and will glo-rify Him immediately'" (John 12:31–32). We see a whole lot of glory going on! The Father glorifies the Son; the Son glorifies the Father. They both receive the title of *Lord*. Not only do we see total equality; we see total unity.

8. With whom do you have difficulty thinking "others first"? Pray about your response to this person, asking the One who is the ultimate model of humility to help you.

---

---

---

## Thursday: Work Out Regularly

1. Prayerfully read today's text:

> **Phil. 2:12** So then, my dear friends, just as you have always obeyed, not only in my presence but even more in my absence, continue working out your salvation with awe and reverence, **2:13** for the one bringing forth in you both the desire and the effort—for the sake of his good pleasure—is God. **2:14** Do everything without grumbling or arguing, **2:15** so that you may be blameless and pure, children of God without blemish though you live in a crooked and perverse society, in which you shine as lights in the world **2:16** by holding on to the word of life so that on the day of Christ I will have a reason to boast that I did not run in vain nor labor in vain.

2. What two specific commands did Paul give in this passage?

_____

_____

3. What did Paul say his readers already do (v. 12)?

_____

_____

_____

4. What did he tell them to continue doing (v. 12)? (Notice he did not tell them to work *for* their salvation.)

_____

_____

_____

5. How were they to do it (v. 12)? Why do you think Paul chose these words?

_____

_____

_____

6. What do you think a worked-out salvation looks like? How would it be characterized?

_____

_____

_____

7. What did Paul give as the reason behind working out one's salvation with awe and reverence (2:13)? The way this is structured, the emphasis falls on the word *God*. How encouraging to note that we exert effort in partnership with the *Almighty*.

_____

_____

_____

8. Why does God bring forth the desire and effort to obey (2:13)?

_____

_____

_____

9. What is the clear command in 2:14? What is its scope? (Some things? A few things?) Note that Paul probably had in mind community living here, not just complaining about stuff like the weather, though that could be included, but complaining *against each other*.

_____

_____

_____

10. What reasons does Paul give for the command here (2:15)?

_____

_____

_____

11. With whom are you most tempted to grumble and argue? Why?

_____

_____

_____

12. Spend some time offering prayers of repentance and petition, asking God to help you live as a person with "outworked" salvation, who promotes unity rather than fussing and fighting.

## FRIDAY: POURED OUT

1. Prayerfully read today's scripture:

**Phil. 2:17** But even if I am being poured out like a drink offering on the sacrifice and service of your faith, I am glad and rejoice together with all of you. **2:18** And in the same way you also should be glad and rejoice together with me.

**2:19** Now I hope in the Lord Jesus to send Timothy to you soon, so that I too may be encouraged by hearing news about you. **2:20** For there is no one here like him who will readily demonstrate his deep concern for you. **2:21** Others are busy with their own concerns, not those of Jesus Christ. **2:22** But you know his qualifications, that like a son working with his father, he served with me in advancing the gospel. **2:23** So I hope to send him as soon as I know more about my situation, **2:24** though I am confident in the Lord that I too will be coming to see you soon.

**2:25** But for now I have considered it necessary to send Epaphroditus to you. For he is my brother, coworker and fellow soldier, and your messenger and minister to me in my need. **2:26** Indeed, he greatly missed all of you and was distressed because you heard that he had been ill. **2:27** In fact he became so ill that he nearly died. But God showed mercy to him—and not to him only, but also to me— so that I would not have grief on top of grief. **2:28** Therefore I am all the more eager to send him, so that when you see him again you can rejoice and I can be free from anxiety. **2:29** So welcome him in the Lord with great joy, and honor people like him, **2:30** since it was because of the work of Christ that he almost died. He risked his life so that he could make up for your inability to serve me.

"**Drink offering**" (2:17)—Paul chose Old Testament imagery to encourage his readers. Having already endured suffering for the gospel and knowing the same was happening to the Philippians, he identified with them. Bob Deffinbaugh, a Texas pastor, wrote about this verse in an article published on bible.org: "In today's idiom, Paul would say that his suffering would simply be the 'icing on the cake' of their sufferings. He uses the imagery of Old Testament sacrifices."

What was that imagery? We find the first drink offering in Genesis 35:14, where we read that Jacob set up a stone at the place where he talked to God and then poured liquid as a sacrifice on the stone. In Exodus and Leviticus, we find wine offered to God with oil and meat. In Numbers, we find instructions for animal sacrifices with drink offerings prepared alongside. Then Isaiah speaks of the Messiah pouring out his soul to death (Isa. 53:12). So Paul draws on this sacrifice imagery using "poured out" as a figurative term for one whose life is offered to God.

Diffenbaugh notes, "[Paul] likens their sufferings to the main sacrifice and his sufferings as the lesser sacrifice of the drink offering, offered on top of, or along with, the main sacrifice. He says that he would gladly suffer in this way along with them. (Note the repeated emphasis on 'joy' in these two verses.) Not only does Paul consider it a privilege to suffer with the Philippians; he sees his sufferings as the lesser of the two."

2. If such is the case—if Paul is poured out—what is his attitude about it (v. 17)?

_____

_____

_____

3. Did he rejoice alone (v. 17)? Explain your answer.

_____

_____

_____

4. What did he assume Timothy would have to say about the Philippians once he visited them (v. 19)?

_____

_____

5. Contrast 2:14 and 2:18. What did Paul say they *should* do instead of arguing and grumbling (v. 18)?

_____

_____

_____

6. What was Paul's frustration with everyone remaining with him except Timothy (vv. 20–21)?

_____

_____

7. Summarize your understanding of the relationship between Paul and Timothy based on Philippians 2:19–23. (Note that Paul was sending Epaphroditus back to them, and he wouldn't be returning to Paul in Rome. But Paul hoped to send Timothy round-trip.)

_____

_____

_____

8. What did Paul see as the outcome of his prison sentence (v. 24)? On what did he base his confidence?

_____

_____

9. If your pastor wrote a letter about people in your congregation who concerned themselves with the things of Christ, could he include you on the list? Why or why not?

_____

_____

_____

**"Minister to me in my need"** (2:25)—Paul was not necessarily speaking here of his financial need. He needed human help. "Paul is not referring to the money the Phillippians sent him. This designation of Epahroditus would be extravagant . . . if he had done no more than to bring the Philippians' gift to Paul. '*Your* (emphatic) commissioner . . . and official public servant for my need' means: for my need of a brother, fellow-worker, and fellow-soldier. The Philippians had sent Epaphroditus as their gift to Paul. The word used is not *angelos*, 'messenger' who brings news or a gift, but *apostolos*, 'one sent on a commission' . . . not an assistant of Paul, only of his own accord, but duly commissioned and officially appointed by the Philippian church."[14]

10. How did Paul characterize Epaphroditus's relationship with the Philippian church (v. 26)?

_____

_____

11. Though Paul described death earlier in the book as being "present with Christ," note his response to Epaphroditus's life-threatening illness (27–28).

_____

_____

[14] R. C. H. Lenski. *Saint Paul's Epistle to the Philippians* (Columbus: Wartburg, 1937), 819-820, as cited in George and Dora Winston. *Recovering Biblical Ministry by Women*, (Longwood, FL: Xulon Press, 2003), 431.

12. Paul spoke of "grief on top of grief" (v. 27). To what griefs do you think he was referring? (Note that if Epaphroditus had died, Paul says he would have grieved rather than simply rejoicing that Epaphroditus got to be with Christ. What does this tell you about how we approach emotional pain?)

_____

_____

_____

_____

13. For what two reasons was Paul eager to send Epaphroditus (v. 28)? What do you think was causing his anxiety on Epaphroditus's behalf?

_____

_____

_____

14. What did Paul tell his readers to do and why (vv. 29–30)?

_____

_____

_____

15. Who do you know that, like Epaphroditus, risked his and/or her life to serve someone? How can you honor that person?

_____

_____

_____

A couple of years ago when I was about to have surgery to repair a broken bone, I received pages of pre-op instructions. The one I recall most vividly said, "No food or drink after midnight on the day of the procedure." The surgeon's nurse even called the day before my procedure to make sure I got it: "*NO FOOD OR DRINK AFTER MIDNIGHT.*"

The food part I could stomach, so to speak. The drink part was another matter.

I am probably one of the few adults who sleeps with a sippy cup beside my bed, a point of great amusement for my daughter. That way when I take a drink in the middle of the night while half-comatose, I won't drench myself.

So sure enough, when I awoke the day of surgery, I longed for a cup of java. On the way to the hospital, I gazed with envy at the water bottle my husband keeps in the car. I'd never paid much attention to it, but now it mocked me from its little plastic holder. I thought, "If only I could touch a drop to my tongue."

I thought about when Jesus suffered on the cross. He didn't say, "My wrists hurt where they nailed me to the wood," nor "My back aches where they whipped me to the tissues." He said, "I thirst."

My mind drifted to Lazarus. Not Lazarus of Bethany, whom Jesus raised from the dead, but the other Lazarus, the one enjoying the comforts of heaven while the rich man who'd disregarded him during his life begged for just a touch of water. The rich man spent his resources on himself and received all of his reward on earth.

As I lay in the admitting room that Wednesday morning, all I could think about was thirst. I thought about how Jesus said "Blessed are those who hunger and *thirst* after righteousness, for they shall be satisfied." In a part of the world where water flows freely from in-house faucets, we can miss that Jesus is talking about near obsession. That day, I longed for water. And I wondered what it would look like if I longed for righteousness, if I longed to "work out my salvation," as much as I coveted ice chips.

More than 2.6 billion people—or forty percent of the entire world's population—live every day with the kind of longing I had for a few hours. They lack clear, clean water to quench their thirst and provide basic sanitation facilities. Girls in particular are denied education because their schools lack private, decent sanitation facilities. Instead they must spend their days fetching $H_2O$.

When my family was in Africa, we met fellow Christians who subsist on milk, goat's meat, and animal blood. Yes, animal blood! They have so little access to clean water that they slit a little place on the neck of a sheep or goat and mix the blood with milk to stay hydrated. Ew!

How is it that we are so out of touch with the way so many live? How is it that we are so rich and they are so poor?

"Consider others as more important than yourselves," Paul admonishes his readers (Phil. 2:3).

Remember what Jesus said about giving a cup of water in His name? Are you doing what you can?

**Prayer:** *Father, thank You for Your mercy. Thank You for Your Son and His humility. Help me to be like Him! I need Your supernatural help to look beyond myself alone and care for others' needs. Help me to work out my salvation—to demonstrate externally the reality of the inner change your Spirit has made in my life. Help me not to hoard the riches You've given me, but to share the gospel and to spend my resources caring for others' needs. Grant me the wisdom to know how to live in a way that brings You glory. Help me look to You and, as a result, to see how I might meet the needs of the world, starting with those in my own church, in Jesus name'. Amen.*

**Memorize:** "You should have the same attitude toward one another that Christ Jesus had, who though he existed in the form of God did not regard equality with God as something to be grasped, but emptied himself by taking on the form of a slave, by looking like other men, and by sharing in human nature. He humbled himself, by becoming obedient to the point of death—even death on a cross! As a result God exalted him and gave him the name that is above every name, so that at the name of Jesus every knee will bow—in heaven and on earth and under the earth—and every tongue confess that Jesus Christ is Lord to the glory of God the Father." (Philippians 2:5–11)

# WEEK FOUR

## *Worthless Credentials: Philippians 3*

**Scripture:** You should have the same attitude toward one another that Christ Jesus had, who though he existed in the form of God did not regard equality with God as something to be grasped, but emptied himself by taking on the form of a slave, by looking like other men, and by sharing in human nature. He humbled himself, by becoming obedient to the point of death—even death on a cross! (Phil. 2:5-8)

About a decade ago the families of our church's pastor, youth pastor, and an elder announced that, with the blessing of our remaining leaders, they were moving as a team to plant a new church a thousand miles away. Two of their three homes sold with relative ease in a difficult market, and another family in the congregation bought the remaining one. We hired one of our seminary interns to assume the position of senior pastor and voted to support the moving families until they could get on their feet in their new locale.

The departure of this core group represented a huge loss for those of us remaining. Our church—though average-sized compared with most American churches—was still smaller than 150 people. So the people leaving comprised a major part of our leadership team. Ouch!

Still, we shared their vision. So we sent them with our blessing.

During their last Sunday with us, we both rejoiced and grieved. We felt "sweet sorrow" as we watched these dear friends depart to do meaningful work. We delighted in their passion to spread the good news, yet we mourned the loss of our daily interactions.

After the service, a friend who had endured a number of church splits in previous congregations pulled me aside and said, "So *this* is how it's supposed to work? I had no idea! I've never seen a church lose leaders for a *good* reason. In my experience it's always been because they were fighting." How sad that she'd never seen a church divide so it could multiply.

Sad, but true, isn't it? In the U.S. alone, nearly four thousand churches close their doors each year never to open them again. And while solid doctrine is worth taking a loving stand for, most church fights have nothing to do with theology, particularly not the core doctrines.

Think about it. If we take a few sinners and combine their collective ambitions, competitions, invalidations, and escalations of conflict—we have an unholy mess. And there's only one way to clean it up: through having the mind of Jesus Christ.

What does it mean to have the mind of Christ? As the NET translators rendered it, it means having His attitude. It means we look out not only for our own personal interests but also the interests of others. So, for example, maybe we don't care for hymns, but for those older in the faith, hymns evoke memories of God's faithfulness. Do we really want to rob them of that so we can rock down? And if so, are we really rocking down *in the Spirit?* Or maybe we don't care for Christian rock music. Yet it represents the primary mode of worship for a different generation. Do we want to rob them of that so we can avoid the beat that bothers us?

If anybody had a right to show up and say, "Hey, I'm the Son of God. Bring me a throne and a footstool," it was Jesus. Yet he washed camel poop off his disciples' feet. If anyone had a right to wear a jeweled diadem, it was the One who wore a crown of thorns. Should we who name the name of Christ expect our heads to be crowned with laurels?

Is your church dividing to multiply or splitting to die? And what are you personally contributing to the equation? Would your fellow congregants say you are adding to or dividing the spirit of oneness?

What kind of math characterizes your church, and what can you contribute to its addition? Its multiplication? Perhaps even, for a time, its subtraction—but never its division?

## MONDAY: JOY AND RE-JOY

1. Pray for insight from the Spirit and then read today's verses:

> **Phil 3:1** Finally, my brothers and sisters, rejoice in the Lord! To write this again is no trouble to me, and it is a safeguard for you.
>
> **3:2** Beware of the dogs, beware of the evil workers, beware of those who mutilate the flesh! **3:3** For we are the circumcision, the ones who worship by the Spirit of God, exult in Christ Jesus, and do not rely on human credentials . . .

To understand where Paul's going in this week's verses, we need to remember where we've been. He has urged his readers to seek unity, to lift up each other, to put others first. He has then given Jesus Christ as the ultimate example of humility. (Christ left heaven, took the form of a slave, and died a shameful death because of His humble, others-first priority.) Paul has gone on to mention Timothy—whom he'll send to the Philippians later—as someone who puts the concerns of Christ over his own, as well as Epaphroditus—whom Paul's sending back to them. Though his language has been gentle up to this point, now Paul warns his readers in the strongest words possible about the anti-humility mentality that will destroy them: pride.

**"Finally"** (3:1)—This word in English usually means a preacher is gearing up to make the final point. But as Paul used it, that's not necessarily the intent. It can also have the sense of "furthermore" or "from here on out."

**"Rejoice in the Lord"** (3:1)—Note the object of rejoicing here. Not "rejoice over your circumstances" or even "rejoice that I might come to you soon," But "rejoice *in the Lord*." You'll recall some of the benefits of salvation Paul outlined earlier in the book—encouragement in Christ, comfort provided by love, fellowship in the Spirit, affection, mercy. Difficult circumstances can never take these away. You may remember that when Jesus' disciples realized they had the power to cast out demons, they rejoiced. Yet the Lord corrected them: "Do not rejoice that the spirits submit to you but that your names are written in heaven" (Luke 10:20).

Not only did Paul tell the Philippians to rejoice, but he served as an excellent example of "in the Lord" rejoicing. Remember, he was under house arrest, falsely accused, and preparing to lose the companion that the Philippians sent to help him. But his rejoicing, an act of worship and obedience, didn't depend on his circumstances. And it was based on real truth: A day is coming when all will be made right. His focus on life "in the Lord" leads to contentment.

**"To write this again"** (3:1)—Paul told them a few verses earlier to rejoice (2:18), and here he repeats himself.

2. Why does Paul give them this imperative *twice* to rejoice (2:18, 3:1)?

_____

_____

_____

3. What do you think he meant by "safeguard"? How can rejoicing be a safeguard?

_____

_____

_____

4. The opposite of rejoicing is grumbling, fussing, complaining. What stories or instances from scripture can you recall in which a lack of contentment led to trouble?

_____

_____

_____

5. What imperative occurs three times in Phil. 3:2?

_____

_____

_____

6. What reasons do you have for rejoicing—the kind of rejoicing Paul commands here?

_____

_____

_____

Paul proceeded by warning against the arrogant joy-stealers. He was speaking of the Judaizers who dogged his ministry. Judaizers claimed to trust Christ for salvation but they added to the gospel of "grace + nothing" by insisting that to be right before God, a Gentile must undergo circumcision and keep Moses' law. Because the Jewish population in Philippi was probably still quite small (recall that in his initial visit to Philippi it consisted of only a small group of women praying), the church there has not experienced ravaging by the Judaizers that other groups like the Galatians have. Yet Paul knew the joy-stealers were on their way, and he sought to immunize his readers with a warning.

7. What three-fold description did he give of these Judaizers (v. 2)?

_____

_____

_____

"**Dogs**" (3:2)—In North America and many countries today, dogs are household pets. But such was not the case in the ancient Near East. Imagine a world without rabies shots, where there's no such thing as an "indoor pet." If you picture something closer to how we view hyenas, you'll understand the unflattering image Paul paints. The irony here is that Jews formerly called Gentiles "dogs." Here Paul defends Gentiles against Judaizing "dogs."

**"Evil workers"** (3:2)—Judaizers perceived themselves to be full of good works. Paul contradicted such thinking by stressing that a focus on externals is actually evil.

**"Those who mutilate the flesh"** (3:2)—The word for "circumcision" and the word "to mutilate" come from the same root. So Paul made a play on words here, showing how circumcising a Gentile Christian was really mutilating him. (Perhaps the closest we can get in English is the difference between circumcise and excise.)

Notice the force of these images. Paul suddenly went from writing a gentle, kindly-toned letter to powerful negative images and strong warnings. And while most Christians don't face the kind of Judaizers the first-century believers faced, we still encounter thinking that adds "perform good works to be accepted by God" to the gospel of grace.

One of my friends was told after she trusted Christ that she would have to give up wearing pants, wearing lipstick, and would need to attend services every Wednesday night to be right with God. Another was told he couldn't become a police officer because he might have to shoot someone and thus incur God's wrath. Another was told he had to vote a certain way.

Notice how different this is from emphasizing the need to "work out" our salvation. One emphasizes that we must work "for" our salvation or work "for" being right with God. The other emphasizes godly living as an outworking of what's already true of us. The difference is essential. Christian sub-cultures can add many rules to the gospel. It's one thing to limit our freedom for the sake of love; it's another altogether if we do so because we think it gains us standing with God.

8. According to Phil. 3:3 who did Paul consider the true circumcision?

_____

_____

_____

9. What are some human credentials we sometimes equate with spirituality? (I'll get you started with some examples: pastor, missionary, seminary graduate, someone who fasts regularly, someone who prays a lot in public, no body piercings or tattoos, men with short hair, Bible teachers. . .)

_____

_____

10. What does Paul say about such credentials?

_____

_____

_____

## TUESDAY: ULTIMATE "CRED"

Have you ever heard someone who dropped out of school say education isn't important? When someone minimizes the importance of something she doesn't have, it sounds defensive. Yet what if the same words come from a person with a PhD? You can assume that person's pride probably doesn't come from her schooling!

Paul did something similar in Philippians 3. He whipped out the list of Judaizers' standards and demonstrated how he soundly trumped them all. Speaking as one with glittering Jewish credentials, he went on to make the point that those things don't matter. In fact, he even viewed them as "negatives" on the balance sheet.

1. Pray for insight and then read what Paul had to say about himself:

**Philippians 3:4**—though [my credentials] too are significant. If someone thinks he has good reasons to put confidence in human credentials, I have more:

**3:5** I was circumcised on the eighth day, from the people of Israel and the tribe of Benjamin, a Hebrew of Hebrews. I lived according to the law as a Pharisee. **3:6** In my zeal for God I persecuted the church. According to the righteousness stipulated in the law I was blameless. **3:7** But these assets I have come to regard as liabilities because of Christ.

**"Circumcised on the eighth day"** (3:5)—Paul's point here is that he was not some adult convert, late on the scene. He was *born* Jewish, and into a law-abiding family, at that.

My ancestors made their way across the United States (before they were all states) on the Oregon Trail. And we so-called native Oregonians are sometimes overly proud of our heritage, viewing ourselves as superior to the later arrivals ("transplants"). When I moved to Texas in my twenties, I encountered a similar mentality. In Dallas people sport "Native Texan" bumper stickers. And people with lesser pedigrees post apologetic stickers that say, "I wasn't born here, but I got here as fast as I could."

By telling the day of his circumcision, Paul flashed his "native law-abiding Israelite" card. Jewish law required circumcision of a baby boy on the eighth day (Lev. 12:3).

**"Of the tribe of Benjamin"** (3:5)—The tribe of Benjamin inherited Jerusalem in the early division of land (Joshua 18:28), and was the tribe from which Israel's first king, Saul, came (1 Sam. 9:21). Esther's relative, Mordecai, was also a Benjamite (Esther 2:5). The point here? As Jewishness goes, Paul has a fabulous pedigree. In his own words, he was **"a Hebrew of Hebrews"** (3:5).

In this first section of Paul's self-portrait, he described what he was born into. But then he went on to include choices that were within his control.

2. Look at Philippians 3:5-6. What three credentials did Paul list that have to do with his own behavior?

a. When it came to the law (3:5)?

_____

_____

b. When it came to zeal (3:6)?

_____

_____

c. When it came to the law-stipulated righteousness (3:6)?

_____

_____

3. Now put it all together. What's your assessment of Paul's Jewish credentials?

_____

_____

_____

_____

_____

_____

_____

> *"Before his conversion Paul fulfilled the law conspicuously, either through fear of the people or of God himself, even if he may have offended the law in his internal affections. But he was fulfilling the law through fear of punishment, not through love of righteousness.*
> *—AUGUSTINE IN "ON TWO LETTERS OF PELAGIUS," 1.15.*

4. How, in your opinion, did his credentials add credibility to his warning against the Judaizers?

_____

_____

_____

5. Paul provided an impressive list. Yet what was his view of these credentials (3:7)?

_____

_____

_____

6. What reason did he give for his negative assessment (3:7)?

_____

_____

_____

7. What do you think he meant? And why?

_____

_____

_____

## WEDNESDAY: THE LOST AND FOUND

1. Pray for wisdom and insight from the Spirit. Then read the verses we'll explore today:

> **Philippians 3:8** More than that, I now regard all things as liabilities compared to the far greater value of knowing Christ Jesus my Lord, for whom I have suffered the loss of all things—indeed, I regard them as dung!—that I may gain Christ, **3:9** and be found in him, not because I have my own righteousness derived from the law, but because I have the righteousness that comes by way of Christ's faithfulness—a righteousness from God that is in fact based on Christ's faithfulness. **3:10** My aim is to know him, to experience the power of his resurrection, to share in his sufferings, and to be like him in his death, **3:11** and so, somehow, to attain to the resurrection from the dead.

2. Circle the phrase "all things." Notice what both uses have in common in terms of how Paul regarded them.

3. Circle the word "know/knowing" both times it appears in Phil. 3:8–11. Notice the word that follows it in both cases to see exactly the kind of knowledge Paul desired to gain.

4. Picture an accounting balance sheet—that seems to be the metaphor Paul has in mind. On the left, list everything he considers a liability. On the right, list everything he considers of value (3:8):

**Liabilities:**                          **Things of Value:**

_____

_____

_____

_____

_____

_____

5. List as many losses you can think of that Paul suffered since becoming a Christian.

_____

_____

_____

6. What was Paul's assessment of all these losses?

_____

_____

_____

**"Dung"** (3:8)—Greek: *skubala*. Mid-sentence Paul decided that "liabilities" wasn't a strong enough word. What Paul formerly thought gained him favor with God he later counted as dung. Paul chose a vulgar term like the s-word we sometimes see on bumper stickers—*skubala* happens! In a tongue-in-cheek essay titled, "Toward an

Evangelical Theology Of Cussing," one of my colleagues at Dallas Seminary explains Paul's meaning:

> Although many liberal scholars and non-Christians believe the Bible is full of crap, there's actually only one place where the word occurs, though it is often scooped up or covered over by modern English translations.
>
> In Philippians 3:8 Paul tells his readers that all the things of religious value in his former life are regarded to him now as *skubalon*, that is, "crap." While liberals . . . and other heretics may feel obliged to remove "crap" from the Bible by flushing it away with euphemisms such as "rubbish" or "refuse," evangelicals who believe every word is inspired by God (2 Tim. 3:16) should refuse to flush. Instead, we should embrace a translation that conveys the rhetorical effect intended by the author, as crass and base as it may seem to our perhaps overly-pious ears (cf. Eccles. 7:16).
>
> The King James Version had no qualms about translating *skubalon* with a more suitable—though emotively sub-standard—"dung." Only Luther had the guts to translate the noun with *Kot* in his landmark German translation. The problem with translations like "refuse" and "rubbish" in today's idiom is that the recent movement by many towards recycling implies that almost all refuse or rubbish has some value. Likewise, even "dung" could be construed as having usefulness at least as fertilizer. Only a harsher term like "crap" would indicate the utter uselessness that Paul had in mind.
>
> So what's Paul's point? He's certainly not flaunting a vulgar term for the sake of attracting attention. Rather, he's using the strongest language possible to emphasize the worthlessness of his own righteousness. It's gross. P-*ew*! *Dis*-gusting!

7. What did Paul desire to gain in exchange for everything (3:8)?

_____

_____

_____

8. We've considered what Paul lost. Now let's look at the opposite. What did Paul want found (3:9)?

_____

_____

_____

9. Contrast how someone is and is not "found" in Christ based on 3:9.

_____

_____

_____

10. What was Paul's goal according to v. 10–11?

_____

_____

_____

_____

"**To know him**" (3:10)—Certainly Paul knew Christ already in the sense that the apostle placed his faith in Jesus' finished work on the cross. Yet he also saw the ultimate goal of the Christian life to be "to know Christ," which is a process. Notice he didn't say "to know the Bible" or "to get to heaven." The object of the Christian's affections is not even the Word. Or the place where God dwells. Or right living. It's a Person, the Lord Himself. And Paul went on to describe what such "knowing" includes.

"**To experience the power of his resurrection**" (3:10)—Paul saw the Christian life as a process which combines the suffering of Good Friday with the joy of Easter, of dying to self and being raised to new life. In his letter to the Ephesians, Paul described being "in

Christ" as experiencing a resurrection. The Bible doesn't say unbelievers are *dying*; it says they're *dead* in their sins (Eph. 2:5–6). And the same power that raises the lost from deadness is accessible to give victory over sin and the forces of darkness. Paul wants to experience that power in his daily life!

**"To share in his sufferings"** (3:10)—More literally, Paul said he wanted to know the "fellowship" of His (Jesus') sufferings. The word *fellowship* evokes an image of intimacy. We know Christ more deeply through suffering, especially if we suffer on His behalf.

The New Testament teaching on suffering includes the insistence that those who follow Christ should expect to suffer. What a far cry from those who preach a prosperity-focused health-and-wealth gospel! In John 15:20 we read that Jesus said, "Remember the words I spoke to you: 'No servant is greater than his master.' If they persecuted me, they will persecute you also."

A researcher who performed hundreds of interviews with Christians persecuted for their faith under a Communist regime identified some characteristics of those who emerged victorious despite opposition. He observed that they know Jesus; they know the power of prayer and fasting; they can recite large portions of Scripture; they know that their suffering is for Jesus' sake; and they recognize that persecution is normal.

Yet we don't have to wait for all-out persecution to share in Christ's sufferings. Many other forms of difficulty also stretch our faith to the limit: the spouse who keeps the faith as she watches her mate walk out on her; the businessperson who goes bankrupt but still trusts God to provide; the child left orphaned who believes she's not alone. In every trial, we fellowship in His sufferings as we gain perspective on what Christ suffered on our behalf. The Creator was treated as an enemy by humanity. The Son was spat on and cried out asking why the Father abandoned Him on Good Friday.

In appreciating the great price paid for us, we fellowship with Him in His suffering.

**"To be like him in his death"** (3:10)—The wording is passive here—"to be made conformable unto his death." Someone else—God—is doing the work in making us like His Son. And what exactly was Jesus *like* in His death? Submissive. Willing. Silent before accusers. Forgiving rather than vengeful. Focusing on others to the end. And ultimately victorious!

Only by knowing Christ and through resurrection power can we become like this. It goes against everything our warring flesh desires.

**"And so, somehow, to attain to the resurrection from the dead"** (3:10)—Paul's wording here as translated can sound a little bit like he has some doubt about his future resurrection. Yet that doesn't make sense in light of his teaching here and elsewhere. He's just made the point in most emphatic terms that he can't please God by human effort.

Many scholars think the seeming uncertainty Paul expressed here ("if by any means I might attain. . .") came from wondering through exactly what means he would reach his resurrection—whether through the return of Christ or through martyrdom. One way or the other, he expected to see that day. And on that day, he wanted to be able to look back at his life knowing he had made Christ his sole focus and means of standing.

11. Spend time talking to God about what Paul set out as his life goal, and what is also to be the ultimate goal of every Christian—to know Him. Your prayer can start something like this: "Lord, help me know Jesus and the power of His resurrection and the fellowship of His suffering, being made conformable to His death no matter by what means I might attain to the resurrection from the dead. . ."

## THURSDAY: ALREADY BUT NOT YET

1. Pray for wisdom and insight from the Spirit. Then read Philippians 3:12–16.

> **Philippians 3:12** Not that I have already attained this—that is, I have not already been perfected—but I strive to lay hold of that for which Christ Jesus also laid hold of me. **3:13** Brothers and sisters, I do not consider myself to have attained this. Instead I am single-minded: Forgetting the things that are behind and reaching out for the things that are ahead, **3:14** with this goal in mind, I strive toward the prize of the upward call of God in Christ Jesus. **3:15** Therefore let those of us who are "perfect" embrace this point of view. If you think otherwise, God will reveal to you the error of your ways. **3:16** Nevertheless, let us live up to the standard that we have already attained.

2. In these verses, how many times and in what ways did Paul stress that he was not yet perfected (note his use of the passive voice to emphasize that someone else does the perfecting)?

_____

_____

_____

3. What did Paul say he was doing to stay focused on the goal (3:13–14)?

_____

_____

_____

**"Forgetting the things that are behind"** (3:13)—Paul's past included some regrets. Remember, he enthusiastically helped to make Stephen a martyr. Yet he let neither his past failures nor his past accomplishments prevent him from pressing on.

My friend, Dr. Celestin Musekura, whom I mentioned earlier, lost six family members following the genocide in Rwanda. For a long time he didn't even know his mother was still alive. At one point he walked through a refugee camp seeking to find members of his family and members of his former congregation. (He was in seminary overseas when the murders took place.) He met pastors in that camp who told him, "I cannot be accepted." Why? Because some of these pastors had given up their own people to be slaughtered. They started out well— they'd hidden members of warring tribes, which was good. But then the militia from either side came to their homes and said, "Pastor, we know you have Tutsis in the house!" Or "we know you have Tutus in the house! Open the house! We want to kill them. If you do not open the door, we're going to throw grenades at your house and you, and your family, and the people you're hiding are going to be killed." Some of these pastors, rather than face death, had handed over members of their flocks, who were then killed in their own front yards. So the question they were asking Celestin was, "Are we of any use now? Can we be used again by God?"

Other people in that camp had relatives whose pastors had given up their loved ones. So both victims and victimizers were asking questions about forgiveness, either "Can God forgive me?" or "How can I possibly forgive this evil?"

Celestin eventually met those who killed his own family members and chose to forgive. He went on to write his doctoral dissertation on forgiveness and reconciliation, and today governments of war-torn African nations ask him to help them make peace.

Forgetting what lies behind is not at all the same as erasing trauma from our memory. Anyone who has suffered such tragedy knows these memories never disappear. (And, in fact, our memories—good and bad—shape who we are.) Instead, forgetting means treating the offender as if the offense never happened, seeking reconciliation, making restitution wherever possible, and choosing to forgive every time the memory haunts. It includes a refusal to dwell on the injuries of the past.

So often we justify our lack of conformity to Christ by pointing to something in our past: "I can't trust God because my husband deserted me"; "I rage at my kids because my parents were abusive with me"; "My father molested me, so I refuse to trust God as a good father"; "I committed immorality so I can't expect God to bless my intimate life." Paul calls us to move beyond the past and press forward. How? By the power of the resurrection.

4. What things, positive and negative, in your past or in the pasts of those you love weigh you down, keeping you from pressing on toward the goal of knowing Christ?

---

---

---

**"Reaching for those things that are ahead"** (3:13)—Picture a runner with her chest thrown forward reaching out for the ribbon at the finish line. Or the Olympic swimmer stretching fingertips toward the wall that stops the clock. If she wants to win, she can't glance behind her to see if a competitor is gaining on her. She has to keep her focus on what's ahead and strain to reach forward.

5. Olympic runners in Paul's day competed for a wilting crown. What prize did Paul have in mind (3:14)?

_____

_____

6. What distractions keep you from reaching for those things that are ahead? What can be done about them?

_____

_____

_____

7. Do you consider yourself a mature Christian? Why or why not?

_____

_____

**"Those of us who are 'perfect' "** (3:15)—Paul, as he often does, uses _perfect_ as a synonym not for sinless perfection but for _mature._

8. To what point of view was Paul referring in verse 15?

_____

_____

_____

9. How confident was he that he had the right point of view (3:15)?

_____

_____

_____

10. What did Paul exhort/command readers to do in 3:16?

_____

_____

_____

11. Why do you think Paul said on the one hand that he had not yet met the standard, but on the other hand he talked of a standard already attained (3:12, 16)?

_____

_____

_____

12. It is often said that the Christian life is a tension of "already/not yet." We are already resurrected, yet we await the resurrection from the dead. We are not yet perfect, yet we reach for a standard we've already attained. We are not sinless, yet God has declared us righteous. Picture a college student who has finished all her course work and must wait a week for the graduation ceremony. She doesn't hold the diploma, but she has already finished the course. On a separate sheet of paper, write out a prayer, asking God to help you attain maturity and thanking Him that the standard has already been attained on your behalf.

## FRIDAY: THE BIG FATHERLAND

1. Pray for wisdom and insight from the Spirit. Then read Philippians 3:17–21.

> **Philippians 3:17** Be imitators of me, brothers and sisters, and watch carefully those who are living this way, just as you have us as an example. **3:18** For many live, about whom I have often told you, and now, with tears, I tell you that they are the enemies of the cross of Christ. **3:19** Their end is destruction, their god is the belly, they exult in their shame, and they think about earthly things. **3:20** But our citizenship is in heaven—and we also await a savior from there,

the Lord Jesus Christ, **3:21** who will transform these humble bodies of ours into the likeness of his glorious body by means of that power by which he is able to subject all things to himself.

2. What two commands do we find in 3:17?

_____

_____

_____

3. In what ways has Paul been an example of spiritual maturity to the Philippians (and to us)?

_____

_____

_____

4. Who else do you know that's an example of Christlike maturity? Why did you choose this person(s)?

_____

_____

_____

5. Philippians 3:18 begins with the word "for." And here it operates like the word "because." Why did Paul conclude that his readers should imitate him as well as others who are striving to know Christ?

_____

_____

_____

6. What was Paul's attitude about the "enemies of the cross of Christ" (3:18)?

_____

_____

_____

7. What three-fold description did Paul give of those who were enemies of the cross?

_____

_____

_____

"**Whose god is the belly**" (3:17)—Bear in mind the context here. Remember, Paul was speaking of those who put confidence in the flesh rather than only in Christ. But whether through legalism, as with the Judaizers, or through license, anyone who puts confidence in the flesh rather than Christ alone in a sense worships him- or herself. We tend to overlook gluttony and focus solely on sexual sins when we think of "sins of the flesh." Yet food was then and is now scarce in many areas of the world, and hunger is a real social problem. When we overindulge in food we take from someone in need, whether directly or indirectly. Remember that the man who wrote this metaphor had suffered hunger. Their appetites dictated what they did.

"**They exult in their shame**" (3:17)—A mark of a decadent person is bragging about what he or she should want to conceal. Think of movie stars and politicians publishing books about their exploits. In Paul's case the legalistic Judaizers preened themselves about circumcision. Paul was not saying they should be ashamed of their bodies, but rather they should be ashamed about placing spiritual confidence in a mark on their bodies to give them standing before God.

"**They think about earthly things**" (3:17)—Again a person whose mind is fixed on earth—whether loving materialism, pursuing fame, flaunting a hot body or anything else that will someday vanish like a vapor—places confidence in the wrong thing. The self-deceived person whose life will end in destruction, according to Paul, worships self, glorifies the shameful, and thinks about me, me, me.

8. Philippians 3:20 begins with the word "but." Paul was flagging a major contrast here. What was he contrasting?

_____

_____

_____

**"Our citizenship is in heaven"** (3:20)—Paul brings up the issue of citizenship again. Clearly he wants his readers to really understand their identity! Despite Philippi's Roman pride, their fatherland is not Rome. Instead, their country is the *big* fatherland—the fatherland of heaven. Ravi Zacharias said, "Like a child who stops sobbing when he is clasped in the arms of his mother, such will be the grip of heaven on our souls."

As I mentioned, my family and I spent some time in Africa last year. We loved worshiping with God's people there and witnessing their unbridled joy and contentment in the midst of poverty. We enjoyed seeing baboons run in front of our car, encountering a family of giraffes, and stopping for a couple of lions in the road. And we liked seeing the beautiful Rift Valley as well as learning to drink Stony (ginger ale on steroids). But still—Africa wasn't home for us. We knew only a few words of Swahili and zero words of the other languages our hosts spoke. The roads were unfamiliar. And customs differed, so we didn't always know the best thing to do in a given situation. Should we hug? Shake hands? Both? Neither? These differences left us feeling a little awkward at times, because we were visitors from the United States of America. We had a wonderful trip, and want to return to Africa, but it also felt great to come home and sleep in our own beds.

Some of my students from Africa feel the same awkwardness about coming to the USA. They wonder what *Charlotte's Web* is. Those learning English as a second language struggle with our inconsistent use of prepositions. And as hard as it may be for us to imagine, not everybody loves pizza!

As Dorothy said, "There's no place like home."

Yet, according to Paul, the comfort of our own beds can deceive us. My own pillow, as good as it feels, isn't truly home. Heaven is home. In the Christian sub-culture, we can pretend we're "happy all the time" in an attempt to project a false spiritual image. And our nation's customs, its favorite TV shows, the behavior of its movie stars, and its focus on Botox, tummy tucks, and teeth three degrees whiter than naturally possible—these should leave us longing for something different, something as familiar to our souls as a loving mother's arms. A place with true substance. A place where there's a Savior we long to know. In contrast with the Judaizers who put confidence in the flesh and earthly applause, Paul wanted his readers to put all their confidence in Christ and His heavenly kingdom.

9. As opposed to "enemies of the cross" (3:18), whose "minds are set on earthly things" (3:19), those who follow Christ crave His appearance and long to be with Him (Rom. 8:23; Gal. 5:5; Titus 2:13; Heb. 9:28). Do you look forward to Jesus' appearance? Why or why not?

_____

_____

_____

10. What do you love about your home?

_____

_____

_____

11. In what ways do you find yourself more attached to earth than you should be?

_____

_____

_____

12. In what ways do you put confidence in the flesh rather than in Christ?

_____

_____

_____

13. Imagine what it will be like to see Christ—finally! Write what you imagine it'll be like:

_____

_____

_____

14. What promise does Paul lay out in 3:21?

_____

_____

15. By what means will God transform our bodies (3:21)?

_____

_____

_____

16. What music helps you focus on heaven? Plan to load your CD player or iPod this week with tunes that help you meditate on your true home.

_____

_____

The writer of the great hymn,"When I Survey the Wondrous Cross," said it well:

> "Forbid it, Lord, that I should boast
> Save in the death of Christ my God.
> All the vain things that charm me most
> I sacrifice them to his blood."

Next time you attend an event where you're introducing yourself or where people are introducing you to their friends, notice what you are "known" for. Is it your relationships—Emily's mother? Mark's wife? Conway's girlfriend? The home-schooling mother of six?

Or are you known by your work—the accountant, the cafeteria lady, the nursery volunteer, the ophthalmologist?

Or maybe it's by your educational credentials—the Sunday school teacher, the seminary graduate, the dorm parent, the college kid, the grad student.

Maybe it's even a key accomplishment—the speaker, the author, the Olympic gymnast, the friend of the president, the TV show producer.

Listen to how you talk about yourself and determine if you're speaking out of desire to know and be known by others (intimacy) or if you're speaking from pride.

My sister, Mary, and her husband, Mark, endured several years of infertility treatment before the adoption of their first daughter. After becoming parents, their doctor located the source of their medical problem, and Mary conceived. But then she miscarried. Following that, she had another positive pregnancy test, and today they have two daughters.

Several years later, Mark took a job in another town. So they began the grueling process of establishing credibility, making new friendships, and finding a new place to worship. Eager to involve herself in ministry, Mary attended the first week of a new women's Bible study at a church she and Mark visited. That morning a group of about ten women introduced themselves, and some of their self-descriptions went something like this:

"Hi, I'm Suzanne and my husband and I have eight kids. We home school."

"Hello, I'm Carmen. We have three kids, but don't worry—we're just getting started. I home school, too."

"I'm Sylvia. We have eleven kids. We home school our children and we eat all natural foods. I have an herb garden."

When it came to her turn, Mary said confidently, "Hi, I'm Mary. We have two girls, we don't home school, and my husband has had a vasectomy." Several women suppressed gasps.

Mary called me later that week to talk about it. She told me, "Afterwards, several women approached me and told me where we could get the vasectomy reversed. Now, correct me if I'm wrong, but isn't the fruit of the Spirit still supposed to be love, joy, peace, patience . . . ?"

There's certainly nothing wrong with having large families, avoiding a lot of preservatives, and making sure our kids get a decent education. And please don't understand me to be picking on home schoolers. Though our daughter goes to a great public school, one of my sisters leads home-schooling seminars. My point is just that sometimes we gauge spiritual maturity with the wrong list of credentials. And getting our credibility from anything but Christ can be a modern form of Judaizing.

I'm inspired by the words of Elizabeth of Hungary, the Christ-following daughter of King Andrew II of Hungary. She was reared in Wartburg Castle in central Germany and at age fourteen married Louis II, King of Thuringia. Within six years he died in a crusade, leaving her with three small children. Still, she had a pedigree that she could have used to her own advantage, yet she used her wealth to help the poor and ill, even building a home for lepers.

During times of famine, Elizabeth opened soup kitchens and sold her jewels to provide for the needy. She was so generous that her brother-in-law tried to seize her estate so she wouldn't give it all away. Though she died at age twenty-four, a quote from her wise young lips has endured: "Here, before my eyes, is my God and my King, the mild and merciful Jesus, crowned with sharp thorns; shall I, who am only a vile creature, remain before him crowned with pearls, gold and precious stones, and by my crown mock his?"

Elizabeth understood that sometimes one's human credentials can be a mockery to Christ. Yet those of us who know Him as our Savior should seek to be known by our key credential: "The Son of God stepped down from his royal throne and became a servant for me." What could possibly be more impressive than that?

**Pray:** *Lord Christ, I love You imperfectly. Help me to love You more, to think on heavenly values rather than the stuff of earth, to put my spiritual confidence in Your finished work for me rather than in my own imperfect spiritual efforts. Help me not only to know You, but to want to know You more than anything else in my life. Change my heart to make You and what You value my consuming passions rather than my own stomach or flesh or earthly values. Form and transform me to look eagerly for Your return, to anticipate that day when I will finally look into Your face and see for myself the One who took my place. Thank You that I don't have to earn favor with God—that all God's favor toward You is credited to me because of Your work. Amen.*

**Memorize:** "My aim is to know him, to experience the power of his resurrection, to share in his sufferings, and to be like him in his death, and so, somehow, to attain to the resurrection from the dead" (Phil. 3:10–11).

# Week Five

## The Secret: Philippians 4

**Scripture:** Not that I seek the gift itself, but I seek for the profit which increases to your account. (Phil. 4:17)

For years my favorite television show was the nightly news. As you can imagine, my teenage daughter considered this yet one more sign of my dorkdom (singing in the car and moving to the beat being others). But a couple of years ago during the holidays when my mom visited, she asked if I ever watched Home and Garden TV (HGTV). I told her I preferred to avoid seeing shows about how I could redo the house with money I lacked. But then she pointed out that shows on the H/G Channel have zero sex, violence, or profanity. She had me there. Not only was I tired of hearing about murders; I also despised all the Viagra and Cialis commercials. So I decided to give HGTV a try.

Now I'm hooked. And among my favorite shows is one in which kids arrange for their parents to get room makeovers for those 1960s paneled basements or their 1970s shag carpet. The grown-up offspring participate in doing the work, and when they're finished, they have a big "reveal" for their folks. One episode in particular grabbed my heart. Some daughters got together and nominated their parents for a new kitchen because their mom always cooked for huge family gatherings in a teeny, long-outdated space. That part the parents knew about. But then the hosts threw in a basement redo as an additional surprise.

Now here's the part I really loved—the dad wept. But not, he said, because he received a beautiful kitchen and basement. Rather, his deepest joy came in seeing the kinds of girls he had raised—young women who would think of their mother and work so hard to benefit her. "They're good girls," he said, blinking misty eyes. Though that dad benefited from his daughters' goodness, his deepest delight was not in the home improvements but in the "heart" behind their gift.

Paul had similar joy over the Philippians. But his went even further. He benefited from their gifts, true. He was glad for their financial support and for the help of Onesimus, whom they had sent. Yet his greatest joy was not in the benefits themselves but in what these gifts revealed—the character and priorities of their senders. Beyond that, Paul rejoiced in knowing how much God would reward the Philippians as a result. His readers demonstrated by their actions that they would rather sacrifice so Paul could spread the gospel than spend their resources on their own comfort.

Two years ago I had an experience that brought home this concept to me. I had a nasty fall head-first down nine stairs in my house that required eighteen months, two surgeries, and wheelchair time to recover. Following one of those surgeries, our church (of about 75 members) provided meals for my family for two weeks. Then three. After that we told them they could stop. But they insisted through week four. And five. Then six. The Body of Christ gave us the help we requested and went on to double it. What a great help it was!

Certainly we benefited from all the marinara, enchiladas, and turkey as well as the homemade bread and chocolate pies. And my husband appreciated not having to cook. His mother also had surgery during that time, so he was working full-time and taking care of both of us in the evenings.

Yet even better than the delicious food was what those meals said about our church family and the eternal reward they would accrue for their generosity. Instead of seeking their own convenience, the Body of Christ expressed through their actions that they understood sacrificial love. And I thought of Paul's words: "You have done well to share with me in my present difficulty. . . . What I want is for you to receive a well-earned reward because of your kindness. At the moment I have all I need—more than I need! I am generously supplied with the gifts you sent me—they are a sweet-smelling sacrifice that is acceptable to God and pleases Him" (see Phil. 4).

When we're generous with others in Christ's body, we express something of our love for the Father. When we give sacrificially, we do more than benefit the recipients. We reveal our priorities. Our care. Our faith. And we lay up a future reward in heaven.

With whom can you be generous with your resources today?

## MONDAY: MIND THE GAP

Pray for the Spirit to grant you insight. Then read today's verses—some of the best known and loved in Philippians:

> **Philippians 4:1** So then, my brothers and sisters, dear friends whom I long to see, my joy and crown, stand in the Lord in this way, my dear friends!
>
> **4:2** I appeal to Euodia and to Syntyche to agree in the Lord. **4:3** Yes, I say also to you, true companion, help them. They have struggled together in the gospel ministry along with me and Clement and my other coworkers, whose names are in the book of life.
>
> **4:4** Rejoice in the Lord always. Again I say, rejoice! **4:5** Let everyone see your gentleness. The Lord is near! **4:6** Do not be anxious about anything. Instead, in every situation, through prayer and petition with thanksgiving, tell your requests to God. **4:7** And the peace of God that surpasses all understanding will guard your hearts and minds in Christ Jesus.
>
> **4:8** Finally, brothers and sisters, whatever is true, whatever is worthy of respect, whatever is just, whatever is pure, whatever is lovely, whatever is commendable, if something is excellent or praiseworthy, think about these things. **4:9** And what you learned and received and heard and saw in me, do these things. And the God of peace will be with you.

2. What evidence of Paul's affection for the Philippians do you find in 4:1? Why do you think he felt this way?

---

---

---

**"My joy and crown"** (4:1)—The word *crown* here is not the one used for royal diadems but rather wreaths of victory or glory. And notice that Paul doesn't speak of the Philippians as his *future* crown. (Paul often refers to heavenly rewards as crowns.) Rather, these people *are* his joy and crown. Already. Presently. Blessings can crown the head of the righteous (Prov. 10:6), and a woman of noble character is a crown to her husband (12:2). In the same way, the Philippians are Paul's "pride and joy."

**"Stand in the Lord in this way"** (4:1)—Like soldiers, believers are to stand, and we stand *in Him*. What did Paul have in mind when he said in *this* way? To find out, we have to look back at the previous context. Here's what he said: "[The Lord Jesus Christ] will transform these humble bodies of ours into the likeness of his glorious body *by means of that power by which he is able to subject all things to himself*." So the way believers stand in the Lord is through the transforming, reigning, resurrection power of the Lord Jesus Christ.

**"I appeal to Euodia and to Syntyche to agree in the Lord"** (4:2)—Paul was probably using a play on words on both the names Euodia and Syntyche to make his point for the whole church. The former sounds exactly like the Greek word *euodia* ("good smell") that Paul used sixteen verses later, ironically implying that Euodia should live up to being a pleasant aroma. *Syntyche* has the prefix *syn-*. And Paul uses fifteen *syn*-prefix terms in the Book of Philippians, emphasizing partnership and unity (an English parallel might be emphasizing "synch" and "synergy" along with instructions to a woman named Syndy.) In fact, he clusters words with the syn-prefix in the next verse.

One scholar summarizes, "It is not too much to say that Philippians fairly shouts forth the importance of Euodia and Syntyche in regard to the past and present of the church at Philippi. Factors ranging from beautiful literary artistry to subtle puns all underline their prominent roles in both the joyful and not so happy times of that congregation. If anything, calling attention to their present problem-causing status (4:2–3; see 2:2–4) only serves to indicate how crucial these two women are. . ."[15]

I've heard a number of sermons in which preachers emphasized the gender of Euodia and Syntyche, adding the suggestion that these two disagreed because they were women "and," these preachers added, "you know how females can be." Yet Paul and Barnabas had a sharp disagreement over whether to take John Mark with them (Acts 15:39), and I've never heard anyone conclude, "Males can be that way. You know what testosterone poisoning can do." Neither gender has a corner on the sin market. The reality: *Humans* can be this way!

What's far more interesting to note in this section of Philippians is Paul's description of the women and his appeal, which is a lesson for us all. He writes, "They have struggled together in the gospel ministry along with me and Clement and my other coworkers, whose names are in the book of life." These women were Paul's co-workers. They were otherwise mature in their faith, and Paul was convinced of their salvation. (If we note anything about gender here, it should be that Paul worked in partnership with women for the sake of the gospel, a rather revolutionary concept at the time.) We see from Paul's words that even mature believers sometimes have deep disagreements, and their relational difficulties can affect the entire church. Yet their conflict doesn't mean they're not Christians.

Note the kind of agreement Paul urged these two to have—agreement *in the Lord*. He's not just speaking of a compromise where both begrudgingly give in. Nor was he saying that the women have to be of the same opinion. Instead, he was appealing to them to find a place of Christian unity, especially because their disagreement was affecting a wide circle. He also called on a third party, a "true companion" whose identity we don't know, but whom his readers would have known, to help them.

A number of years ago a woman in our church and our pastor had a sharp disagreement over worship styles. Both had legitimate concerns. But their points of view differed so radically that the woman and her husband felt led to leave the church. Still, she and the pastor were committed to coming to a place of unity before they completely parted ways. So along with their spouses they asked my husband and

---

[15] A. Lloyd Luter, Jr., "Partnership in the Gospel: The Role of Women in the Church at Philippi," *Journal of the Evangelical Theological Society*, (Lynchburg, VA: JETS [Electronic edition by Galaxie Software]), 1998.

me to join them for a tough conversation. That evening both exhibited humility and a willingness to put the other's needs first. And as we closed our time together, we found the closest thing to communion food available—juice and tortillas—and shared the Lord's Supper together. Ultimately the pastor and that woman did not agree in the sense that they held the same opinion on the subject. Yet they agreed *in the Lord*. And today they remain friends, encouraging each other and praying for one another.

Disagreements are inevitable. Being of the same mind (Christlike) is not the same as being of the same opinion (agreeing about everything). The church is a diverse group. That's part of its beauty! Yet our opinions and views must take a back seat to our mindset of humility and our commitment to oneness.

3. Is there someone with whom you need to come to a place of Christlike unity?

_____

_____

_____

4. Does someone else need your help coming to a place of unity? If so, who? And how can you help?

_____

_____

_____

**"Rejoice in the Lord always. Again I say, rejoice! (4:4)**—Paul began by telling his readers twice to rejoice (2:18; 3:1). Yet here he is again. And yet again. Rejoicing is an essential quality for those who believe their names are written in the book of life, who believe the Lord is near, and that God is just, in control, answers prayer, and will provide! And notice the frequency of rejoicing—always. So it's not dependent on circumstances. Paul seems to anticipate their response: "What? Always? Are you sure?"

What does he say? *"Again* I say, rejoice!"

5. Would you say you're known more for rejoicing or fussing? Spend a few moments praying that God would help you be a joy-filled person.

**"Let everyone see your gentleness. The Lord is near!"** (4:5)— Have you ever noticed how often Christians have a reputation for what they're *against* rather than what they're *for*? Any time someone asks my friend for his opinion, he jokes, "I'm a [insert denominational affiliation], so I'm against *everything*!" Some years ago a couple of Texas seminary students punched each other in the student lounge over a fine point of doctrine!

If we are known for something, it should not be for our confrontational interactions but rather our gentleness and peaceableness.

When we see Paul's flow of logic, he probably has public suffering in mind. First, rejoice. Second, don't fight; be gentle. And let everybody see it. This he follows with an encouragement that the Lord is near. He may mean that the Lord never leaves us, or perhaps that Jesus is coming soon. Probably both. In light of God's presence and imminent return, we live like we have a future. We don't have to fight. We can rejoice. No need to worry. Which leads us to the next point:

**"Do not be anxious about anything"** (4:6)—Paul again used words like "always" and "anything," which set a high standard. How can we be "un"-anxious?

Years ago my husband and I went through a decade of infertility treatment before the adoption of our daughter. And at one point in the process I learned I needed surgery to see if I had endometriosis. Now, I hate surgery. Even if it's considered minor, if it's performed on *me*, that qualifies it as major from my perspective. I was so sure I'd die on the operating table that I changed the beds (so guests coming for my memorial service would sleep on clean sheets) and penned good-bye notes to loved ones in my journal. When I went to my pre-op appointment twenty-four hours before surgery, I asked my doctor—a brother in Christ—to prescribe a sleeping pill. He laughed and asked why, and I told him how stressed out I was. So shaking his head, he smiled and wrote me a script for *one* pill.

I knew what he was thinking. It was pretty silly. So after I arrived home, I took stock of my ridiculous behavior. Where was my trust? My faith?

I pulled out my Bible and meditated on Psalm 91. Moses' words about dwelling in the secret place of the Most High and abiding in the shadow of the Almighty soothed me, and I cast my cares on Him. And that night I slept fine, guarded by an inexplicable, pill-free peace.

**"Instead, in every situation, through prayer and petition with thanksgiving, tell your requests to God"** (4:7)—Apparently there's no circumstance so minor or silly that it falls outside of "every" situation. And how are we to tell God our requests? With prayer, petition, and thanksgiving. Thanksgiving falls right in line with Paul's constant reminder to rejoice. If we only ask and never thank or praise, what does that say about us? Yet some of us praise but feel awkward *asking*. Paul calls us to both.

6. List five things for which you're thankful. Spend some time praising God for these.

A.

_____

_____

B.

_____

_____

C.

_____

_____

D.

_____

_____

E.

_____

_____

7. For what are you anxious? List concerns on your heart. Then spend some time casting these on the Lord, making petition, or request, with thanksgiving.

_____

_____

_____

"And the peace of God that surpasses all understanding will guard your hearts and minds in Christ Jesus" (4:7)—The peace here is the peace God produces. Such peace is the promise that comes with the command to pray with thanksgiving. God's peace, like a military officer sent as a peacekeeper, will stand over the heart and mind, protecting the one who prays from the worry-forces outside that can twist with hurricane force. Why does such peace surpass understanding? Because it makes no sense humanly speaking. Our friend, John, lost his daughter to cancer a number of years ago, and this is the verse that has sustained him. How does a father survive such anguish? Only through prayer and the Spirit bringing supernatural, logic-defying peace.

8. Describe a time when you had such inexplicable peace from God.

_____

_____

_____

"Finally, brothers and sisters, whatever is true . . . worthy of respect . . . just . . . pure . . . lovely . . . commendable . . . excellent or praiseworthy, think about these things" (4:8). We become what we think. Garbage in/garbage out. Good stuff in/good stuff out. With what do you fill your mind? We waste precious time if we always mentally camp on stuff that will pass away such as clothing, physical beauty, the latest movie stars and their marriages and divorces; or how to get ahead at work; or how upset we are with spouses, kids, coworkers, fellow church members. We also grow callous to pain if we fill our minds with a steady diet of murder, rape, and injustice. Rather, our minds should dwell on justice, honor, truth, high standards, and goodness.

Does that mean we can't watch CNN or the Fox News Channel or view the daily news online or in newspapers? After all reporters speak of murders, people trampled to death, earthquakes, even beheadings.

I think we often misunderstand Philippians 4:10. Some conclude from it that we must shelter ourselves and our kids from all ungodly outside influences to keep our minds on what's good. In so doing, we grow painfully out of touch and unable to speak truth regarding those situations.

If someone likened the evil deeds of God's people to a harlot going after men with genitals the size of donkeys, we might think that's an unholy violation of Paul's instructions here in Philippians. Yet that's exactly what the prophet Ezekiel did (see Ezekiel 23). Meditating on what's true and right—God's Word—includes knowing and understanding such passages.

The solution, rather than completely shielding ourselves, is to assess each thing we view or discuss or consider *from God's perspective*. How does God view harlotry? How does God view earthquakes and starvation? What is a just response to murder? To beheadings? Considering God's perspective on these is thinking about what's true and right, even if the subject matter is dark. If a movie has us rooting for evil to win, for lawbreakers to prevail, that's unjust. But if a story shows evil to be evil in all its darkness, evoking in us a desire for right to rule, that perspective falls in line with God's assessment.

Do you ever watch TV commercials and cast your eyes heavenward, exclaiming, "Oh puh-lease"? I think that is how this verse is supposed to look in relation to us when we encounter what's untrue, unworthy of respect, unjust, impure, and shameful. We will inevitably encounter such things. And when we do, we should evaluate them by the standards laid out here.

But we also must actively fill our minds with what is lovely. And what is more lovely than our Savior? Puritan theologian Richard

Baxter in *The Saints' Everlasting Rest* (1650) wrote, "It is but right that our hearts should be on God when the heart of God is so much on us. If the Lord of glory should stoop so low as to set His heart on sinful dust, methinks we should easily be persuaded to set our hearts on Christ and glory and ascend to Him in our daily affections, who so much condescends to us."[16]

Any time, but especially in times of turmoil, it's helpful to read God's word, to load the CD player with the Bible on audio, to replace stressful thoughts with God's truth.

9. With what do you fill your mind? Be specific. What do you passively and actively let in (internet, magazines, conversations, reading, movies, TV, radio, Bible reading, etc.)?

_____

_____

_____

10. Evaluate the stuff that fills your mind against the standard laid out in 4:10. How are you doing? What improvements can you make?

_____

_____

_____

**"And what you learned and received and heard and saw in me, do these things"** (4:9)—What had the Philippians seen of Paul? Making the gospel priority one. Singing when persecuted. Rejoicing in suffering. Teaching sound doctrine. Devoted to prayer.

Sometimes people say, "Don't follow a man; follow God." Yet Paul says it's okay to imitate people who do a good job of following God. Paul lived in such a way that he could tell people to emulate the example he set.

---

[16] Richard Baxter. *The Saints' Everlasting Rest* as recorded in Baille, Day 310.

11. What of Paul's behavior and attitudes do you most need to imitate in this season of your life?

_____

_____

_____

**"And the God of peace will be with you"** (4:9)—Again, Paul promises peace. God's serene presence was available to stabilize his readers as they imitated him. The Philippians needed to imitate Paul in his perseverance through persecution. And the God of peace, he promised, will give them calm in exchange for anxiety and peace in exchange for stress. Even if they were to lose their lives for the gospel, having the assurance of God's presence could give these believers peace in the moment—what great promises!

## TUESDAY: THE SECRET

1. Ask the Spirit to give you insight. Then read today's verses:

**Philippians 4:10** I have great joy in the Lord because now at last you have again expressed your concern for me. (Now I know you were concerned before but had no opportunity to do anything.) **4:11** I am not saying this because I am in need, for I have learned to be content in any circumstance. **4:12** I have experienced times of need and times of abundance. In any and every circumstance I have learned the secret of contentment, whether I go satisfied or hungry, have plenty or nothing. **4:13** I am able to do all things through the one who strengthens me. **4:14** Nevertheless, you did well to share with me in my trouble.

**"I have great joy in the Lord"** (4:10)—Note what kind of joy Paul has—it's joy _in the Lord_. Paul saw the Philippians' provision as ultimately coming from the hand of God, and the joy he felt was spiritually motivated.

**"Again expressed your concern for me"** (4:10)—Paul's joy here was connected to God's provision through his readers. The Philippians had expressed their concern in tangible ways.

**"I am not saying this because I am in need"** (4:11)—Yet Paul didn't want them to think his contentment came from having his needs met. Nor was he hinting that he wanted more.

**"For I have learned to be content in any circumstance"** (4:11)—"For" introduces the reason for Paul's statement. It's not that he had zero needs. Rather, no matter what his needs were, he was content. Notice the word "any" which qualifies what circumstance. Paul mastered the art of contentment.

2. Are you content? Why or why not?

_____

_____

_____

_____

3. In what circumstances do you have the most difficulty being content?

_____

_____

_____

_____

**"I have experienced times of need and times of abundance"** (4:12)—Have you ever noticed that sometimes we have a tougher time being content in times of abundance than in times of need? Think of the children of Israel fussing about manna. When I compare my own attitudes with the contentment I saw in my African brothers and sisters, I see that many are more content with little than I am with plenty!

Paul said he knew what it was like to live both with need and with abundance. And then he went on to say he'd mastered being content in *both* situations.

4. Do you find that for you it's easier to be content in times of want or in times of plenty? Explain your answer.

_____

_____

_____

**"In any and every circumstance I have learned the secret of contentment, whether I go satisfied or hungry, have plenty or nothing"** (4:12)—Even though he already said in v. 11 that the scope of his contentment included "*any* circumstance," here Paul reiterates that his mastery includes "any and every circumstance." Put it together and you can see how strongly he's emphasizing *every single* situation. This is particularly amazing in light of what he said elsewhere about his circumstances:

> **2 Corinthians 11:24** Five times I received from the Jews forty lashes less one. **11:25** Three times I was beaten with a rod. Once I received a stoning. Three times I suffered shipwreck. A night and a day I spent adrift in the open sea. **11:26** I have been on journeys many times, in dangers from rivers, in dangers from robbers, in dangers from my own countrymen, in dangers from Gentiles, in dangers in the city, in dangers in the wilderness, in dangers at sea, in dangers from false brothers, **11:27** in hard work and toil, through many sleepless nights, in hunger and thirst, many times without food, in cold and without enough clothing. **11:28** Apart from other things, there is the daily pressure on me of my anxious concern for all the churches.

So what is the secret of Paul's contentment? I believe the previous phrase ("I have learned the secret of contentment") should end with a colon, not a period, (there's no punctuation in Koine Greek) so we catch that his secret is this:

**"I am able to do all things through the one who strengthens me"** (4:13)—That's it! How can he be content? What's his secret? It's Christ's strength! Paul can do all things, even the seemingly impossible task of rejoicing in every situation, and being truly okay with it through the power of the One who gives him strength. Paul's not bragging in his ability. He's boasting in the Lord. His secret is *Christ and His resurrection power.*

We have access to this spiritual secret as well. So we can be content in all things.

**"Nevertheless, you did well to share with me in my trouble"** (4:14)—Still, Paul emphasized that even though he was all right with hunger and cold and thirst because of Christ's strength helping him, the Philippians did well to take care of him in his difficulty.

5. Is there someone you know who is content in difficulty but who could, nevertheless, benefit from your help? What can you do?

_____

_____

_____

6. Are you experiencing Christ's power to give you contentment in your present circumstances?

_____

_____

_____

As I write this, my family and I have just returned from the funeral of our friend Brian, a forty-five-year-old who died of brain cancer, leaving behind a wife and three young kids. He was a kind, fun-loving, ethical, passionate-about-Christ believer whom his brother never once heard complain through years of chemo, radiation and bad news. I sat next to a church elder at the service, and his first words to me were, "This is the kind of situation that makes me wonder 'God, What are you doing? Those kids are so young. They need a dad.' "

At the end of the hour, Brian's big brother—this man who just lost his beloved "buddy" and "hero"—told everyone on behalf of the family, "We do grieve. Yet you must know, it is well with our souls."

Only the power of Christ can bring that settled sense of wellness in the midst of such excruciating pain.

7. Are you living in such a way that the only possible explanation for your life is the power of Christ?

_____

_____

_____

8. Cast your cares on Him and ask the Spirit to empower you, despite emotional pain and trauma and physical need, to be content in Him.

## WEDNESDAY: SEEKING CREDIT

1. Prayerfully read Philippians 4:15–23, our final verses of study in the book.

> **Philippians 4:15** And as you Philippians know, at the beginning of my gospel ministry, when I left Macedonia, no church shared with me in this matter of giving and receiving except you alone. **4:16** For even in Thessalonica on more than one occasion you sent something for my need. **4:17** I do not say this because I am seeking a gift. Rather, I seek the credit that abounds to your account. **4:18** For I have received everything, and I have plenty. I have all I need because I received from Epaphroditus what you sent—a fragrant offering, an acceptable sacrifice, very pleasing to God. **4:19** And my God will supply your every need according to his glorious riches in Christ Jesus. **4:20** May glory be given to God our Father forever and ever. Amen. **4:21** Give greetings to all the saints in Christ Jesus. The brothers with me here send greetings. **4:22** All the saints greet you, especially those who belong to Caesar's household. **4:23** The grace of the Lord Jesus Christ be with your spirit.

The Philippians had a long history of taking good care of Paul. In fact back in the early years of his time in Macedonia, they were the only church to provide materially for him. Thessalonica lies about ninety miles from Philippi over rough terrain, and more than once the church at Philippi sent provision to him there. Keep in mind they had no postal service or overnight delivery businesses. Paul reminded them of their past care, but then he emphasized that he wasn't looking for more.

"**Credit that abounds to your account**" (4:17)—Paul used an accounting metaphor to describe the heavenly ledger showing a huge credit that existed—not just in the future but presently—on their account. God rewards such deeds, and because of that Paul's readers had a generous credit, one that "abounds."

1. Does your church have a good reputation for taking care of its ministry workers? Why or why not?

 

 

 

2. Are you personally caring well for people you know who make the gospel a priority and depend on others for support?

 

 

 

3. Take a look at your checkbook and your calendar. Do they demonstrate your belief that God rewards generosity?

 

 

 

4. What three-fold description does Paul give of the Philippians' generosity (4:18)?

 

 

 

Think of the aroma of a summer barbeque with top sirloin on the grill. That's the sort of fragrance Paul imagines. He has shifted from a business or accounting metaphor to a fragrance metaphor.

5. What are some of your favorite fragrances? In what ways is generosity like a wonderful aroma?

_____

_____

_____

6. What does Paul believe is God's assessment of the Philippians' care for him (4:18)?

_____

_____

_____

7. What does Paul promise, as a result (4:19)?

_____

_____

_____

**"My God will supply your every need"** (4:19)—Sometimes we claim this verse as a promise that God will supply every Christian's material need—an indication that we'll never go hungry or be in want. Yet it's important to note the context in which Paul said it. In the process of affirming the Philippians for their sacrificial gifts to him, both financial and personnel, and because of the faith they have exercised in doing so, he is confident God will take care of them. It's a variation on "give and it will be given to you." And the scope of needs goes beyond financial to include "your every need."

Sadly, many of us consider ourselves to be sacrificing if we put anything at all in the offering at church. Yet Ron Sider, known for speaking on behalf of the poor, makes this chilling observation: "The level of Christian giving has gone down over the last thirty years precisely as our income has gone up. Evangelical giving, in particular, has dropped dramatically, from 6.15 percent of income in 1968 to 4.27 percent in 2001. The richer evangelicals have become, the smaller percentage of their income they have given. . . Academic studies show that houses today on average are twice as large as forty years ago. For evangelicals in the richest society in human history to give less and less as they grow richer and richer until they give well below one-half of a tithe is not, I think, something Jesus or Amos would seek to excuse."[17]

Along those lines, my friend, Heather, who established an orphanage in Kenya, wrote me this: "I looked up the Sodom passage in Ezekiel 16:49. . . 'Now this was the sin of your sister Sodom: She and her daughters were arrogant, overfed and unconcerned; *they did not help the poor and needy. . .*' In light of how many times I've heard a sermon on Sodom and Gomorrah and how few times I've heard this aspect incorporated into it, I'd say that our culture may have missed a little somethin'-somethin' in the Book."

While in Africa, my family and I visited a number of remote villages. The poverty level astounded us. We realized that even if my husband and I were out of work for the rest of our lives, between the church, our families, and the government, we would still have clothing, clean water, and enough food to keep us from starving–more than we could say for most of the African people we met who were working hard.

One brother told of how God stopped him from eating concrete mix as a kid. He had not eaten for six days and found powder he thought might quell his hunger pangs, so he mixed it with water and prepared to eat it when he was interrupted by a knock at the door. He hid the mix under the bed and opened the door to find a man with some groceries. When the boy returned and removed the mixture, he found it hardened. He later heard on the radio that two children had died from eating concrete. At that point, he realized God had His hand on his life.

---

[17] Sider, Ron. "Letters," *Books and Culture: A Christian Review* 14, no. 3 (May/June 2008): 5–7.

One of my former students wrote a few days later from South Africa telling me of a church there that holds a monthly service where *everyone* who owns more than one shirt is asked to bring anything they own in excess of one and to give it to somebody with none.

8. Has God met all your needs?

_____

_____

_____

9. Describe your view of what a generous Christian looks like.

_____

_____

_____

10. Evaluate yourself by the standard of generosity you've just laid out. How are you doing?

_____

_____

_____

"**According to his glorious riches in Christ Jesus**" (4:19)— God draws from the account containing the glorious riches of Christ to repay the generous. So he has infinitely deep pockets! What a great God! The thought evokes a doxology:

"**May glory be given to God our Father forever and ever. Amen**" (4:20)

Paul concludes with greetings from the spiritual family in Rome, starting with his co-workers, "**the brothers with me here,**" followed by "**all the saints.**" But then he specifically narrows it to, "**especially those who belong to Caesar's household.**" This would include more than Caesar's immediate family, extending to all who serve him, slave and free. Because of Philippi's status as a Roman city, some of the believers of "Caesar's household" may have even been familiar to members of the Philippian church.

**"The grace of the Lord Jesus Christ be with your spirit"** (4:23)—Paul ends where he started, wishing for the Philippians the spiritual "grace of the Lord Jesus Christ." Between the two bookends of grace at the beginning and end, we have seen what that grace looks like lived out in the life of one who trusts in God and those who partner with him in ministry.

Write out a prayer of thanksgiving to God for His abundant provision for you in every way.

_____

_____

_____

_____

_____

_____

## THURSDAY: YOU, THE SCRIBE

One afternoon as I was on my way to meet a friend, I stopped at a red light. A semi-truck driver was having trouble navigating the intersection and needed all other drivers to back up to give him more room. Unfortunately the woman in the car behind me prevented us from doing so because she was oblivious to the situation. The phone against her ear had her total attention and she never clued in. Is it possible to drive while talking on the phone? Sure. But is the driver as aware of his or her surroundings? No way.

I think the same sort of disengagement sometimes happens when we watch Bible stories on video or read books *about* the Bible. We can get to our destination, but we miss some important details along the way. Sometimes we need to slow down and really pay attention.

In the history of the nation of Israel, God gave some specific instructions to Moses to pass along to the people. Moses recorded God's words in what we know as Deuteronomy. And one of the commands included instruction about what the king was to do with God's law:

> When you come to the land the Lord your God is giving you and take it over and live in it and then say, "I will select a king like all the nations surrounding me," you must select without fail a king whom the Lord your God chooses . . . When he sits on his royal throne *he must make a copy of this law* on a scroll given to him by the Levitical priests. It must be with him constantly and he must read it as long as he lives, so that he may learn to revere the Lord his God and observe all the words of this law and these statutes and carry them out. Then he will not exalt himself above his fellow citizens or turn from the commandments to the right or left, and he and his descendants will enjoy many years ruling over his kingdom in Israel (Deut. 17:14–15; 18–20, italics mine).

One of my mentors suggested that I purchase a lined journal and do as the king did—write out the entire Book of Deuteronomy so that I could learn to revere God, observe all the words of His law, and carry them out. It took me about a year of Sundays in one- or two-hour segments to do so, but I finally finished it.

The beauty of the assignment was that it forced me—in our multitasking world—to slow down and chew on all the words. Every. Single. Letter. Because I took my time, I thought more about what I read. I made connections with other truths. And I noticed recurring names and places.

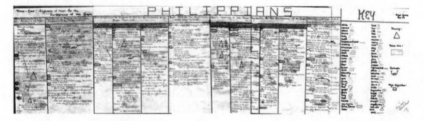

When I was in college, my Pauline Epistles professor assigned a similar project. Each time we studied a book—whether medium-length Philippians or even the longer Book of Acts—he had us write it out longhand on a scroll. First we came up with outlines and headings. Then we made boxes for the headings and beneath them filled in every word from the text. After that we used colored pencils to highlight repeated words and connect them with lines. We circled repeated phrases and meditated on the thoughts as we copied them all out.

I grew in my appreciation for how easy it would have been for a scribe to miss a letter or even an entire line, especially when two lines started with the same word!

Now it's your turn. Spend the next two days simply writing out the Book of Philippians—copying half of the book each day. (No need to outline or chart. Just write it as you would a letter to a friend.) As you do so, chew on Paul's words. Notice how he exalts Christ. Think about how important it was to Paul to spread the gospel. Pray with him the great prayer offered on behalf of the Philippians. Only this time fill in your own name and the names of those you love.

Such slow interaction with God's Word is more than an antidote to save us from the poison of fast times. It's a form of meditation that comes with the rewards promised in Psalm 1 for the one who "meditates day and night." The person who does so, the psalmist said, is "like a tree firmly planted by streams of water, which yields its fruit in its season" (NASB).

> To view the site of ancient Philippi on Google Earth, look for Filippoi-Krinides in Greece at the north end of the Aegean Sea

Even though I've left in the chapter and verse numbers here, I recommend leaving them out in your own version so you get the sense of how the letter flowed without interruption.

Now . . .

1. Pray for insight and enjoy!

**Philippians 1:1** From Paul and Timothy, slaves of Christ Jesus, to all the saints in Christ Jesus who are in Philippi, with the overseers and deacons. **1:2** Grace and peace to you from God our Father and the Lord Jesus Christ!

**1:3** I thank my God every time I remember you. **1:4** I always pray with joy in my every prayer for all of you **1:5** because of your participation in the gospel from the first day until now. **1:6** For I am sure of this very thing, that the one who began a good work in you will perfect it until the day of Christ Jesus. **1:7** For it is right for me to think this about all of you, because I have you in my heart, since both in my imprisonment and in the defense and confirmation of the gospel all of you became partners in God's grace together with me. **1:8** For God is my witness that I long for all of you with the affection of Christ Jesus. **1:9** And I pray this, that your love may abound even more and more in knowledge and every kind of insight **1:10** so that you can decide what is best, and thus be sincere and blameless for the day of Christ, **1:11** filled with the fruit of righteousness that comes through Jesus Christ to the glory and praise of God.

**1:12** I want you to know, brothers and sisters, that my situation has actually turned out to advance the gospel: **1:13** The whole imperial guard and everyone else knows that I am in prison for the sake of Christ, **1:14** and most of the brothers and sisters, having confidence in the Lord because of my imprisonment, now more than ever dare to speak the word fearlessly.

**1:15** Some, to be sure, are preaching Christ from envy and rivalry, but others from goodwill. **1:16** The latter do so from love because they know that I am placed here for the defense of the gospel. **1:17** The former proclaim Christ from selfish ambition, not sincerely, because they think they can cause trouble for me in my imprisonment. **1:18** What is the result? Only that in every way, whether in pretense or in truth, Christ is being proclaimed, and in this I rejoice.

Yes, and I will continue to rejoice, **1:19** for I know that this will turn out for my deliverance through your prayers and the help of the Spirit of Jesus Christ. **1:20** My confident hope is that I will in no way be ashamed but that with complete boldness, even now as always, Christ will be exalted in my body, whether I live or die. **1:21** For to me, living is Christ and dying is gain. **1:22** Now if I am to go on living in the body, this will mean productive work for me, yet I don't know which I prefer: **1:23** I feel torn between the two, because I have a desire to depart and be with Christ, which is better by far, **1:24** but it is more vital for your sake that I remain in the body. **1:25** And since I am sure of this, I know that I will remain and continue with all of you for the sake of your progress and joy in the faith, **1:26** so that what you can be proud of may increase because of me in Christ Jesus, when I come back to you.

**1:27** Only conduct yourselves in a manner worthy of the gospel of Christ so that—whether I come and see you or whether I remain absent—I should hear that you are standing firm in one spirit, with one mind, by contending side by side for the faith of the gospel, **1:28** and by not being intimidated in any way by your opponents. This is a sign of their destruction, but of your salvation—a sign which is from God. **1:29** For it has been granted to you not only to believe in Christ but also to suffer for him, **1:30** since you are encountering the same conflict that you saw me face and now hear that I am facing.

**2:1** Therefore, if there is any encouragement in Christ, any comfort provided by love, any fellowship in the Spirit, any affection or mercy, **2:2** complete my joy and be of the same mind, by having the same love, being united in spirit, and having one purpose. **2:3** Instead of being motivated by selfish ambition or vanity, each of you should, in humility, be moved to treat one another as more important than yourself. **2:4** Each of you should be concerned not only about your own interests, but about the interests of others as well. **2:5** You should have the same attitude toward one another that Christ Jesus had,

> **2:6** who though he existed in the form of God
> did not regard equality with God
> as something to be grasped,
> **2:7** but emptied himself
> by taking on the form of a slave,
> by looking like other men,
> and by sharing in human nature.
> **2:8** He humbled himself,
> by becoming obedient to the point of death
> —even death on a cross!
> **2:9** As a result God exalted him
> and gave him the name
> that is above every name,
> **2:10** so that at the name of Jesus
> every knee will bow
> —in heaven and on earth and under the earth—
> **2:11** and every tongue confess
> that Jesus Christ is Lord
> to the glory of God the Father.

**2:12** So then, my dear friends, just as you have always obeyed, not only in my presence but even more in my absence, continue working out your salvation with awe and reverence, **2:13** for the one bringing forth in you both the desire and the effort—for the sake of his good pleasure—is God. **2:14** Do everything without grumbling or arguing, **2:15** so that you may be blameless and pure, children of God without blemish though you live in a crooked and perverse society, in which you shine as lights in the world **2:16** by holding on to the word of life so that on the day of Christ I will have a reason to boast that I did not run in vain nor labor in vain. **2:17** But even if I am being poured out like a drink offering on the sacrifice and service of your faith, I am glad and rejoice together with all of you. **2:18** And in the same way you also should be glad and rejoice together with me.

**2:19** Now I hope in the Lord Jesus to send Timothy to you soon, so that I too may be encouraged by hearing news about you. **2:20** For there is no one here like him who will readily demonstrate his deep concern for you. **2:21** Others are busy with their own concerns, not those of Jesus Christ. **2:22** But you know his qualifications, that like a son working with his father, he served with me in advancing the gospel. **2:23** So I hope to send him as soon as I know more about my situation, **2:24** though I am confident in the Lord that I too will be coming to see you soon.

**2:25** But for now I have considered it necessary to send Epaphroditus to you. For he is my brother, coworker and fellow soldier, and your messenger and minister to me in my need. **2:26** Indeed, he greatly missed all of you and was distressed because you heard that he had been ill. **2:27** In fact he became so ill that he nearly died. But God showed mercy to him—and not to him only, but also to me—so that I would not have grief on top of grief. **2:28** Therefore I am all the more eager to send him, so that when you see him again you can rejoice and I can be free from anxiety. **2:29** So welcome him in the Lord with great joy, and honor people like him, **2:30** since it was because of the work of Christ that he almost died. He risked his life so that he could make up for your inability to serve me.

2. What stood out to you as you copied from Philippians today?

_____

_____

3. What blessed you as you wrote?

_____

_____

_____

1. Pray for insight. Then copy these verses today:

**Philippians 3:1** Finally, my brothers and sisters, rejoice in the Lord! To write this again is no trouble to me, and it is a safeguard for you.

**3:2** Beware of the dogs, beware of the evil workers, beware of those who mutilate the flesh! **3:3** For we are the circumcision, the ones who worship by the Spirit of God, exult in Christ Jesus, and do not rely on human credentials **3:4**—though mine too are significant. If someone thinks he has good reasons to put confidence in human credentials, I have more: **3:5** I was circumcised on the eighth day, from the people of Israel and the tribe of Benjamin, a Hebrew of Hebrews. I lived according to the law as a Pharisee. **3:6** In my zeal for God I persecuted the church. According to the righteousness stipulated in the law I was blameless. **3:7** But these assets I have come to regard as liabilities because of Christ. **3:8** More than that, I now regard all things as liabilities compared to the far greater value of knowing Christ Jesus my Lord, for whom I have suffered the loss of all things—indeed, I regard them as dung!—that I may gain Christ, **3:9** and be found in him, not because I have my own righteousness derived from the law, but because I have the righteousness that comes by way of Christ's faithfulness—a righteousness from God that is in fact based on Christ's faithfulness. **3:10** My aim is to know him, to experience the power of his resurrection, to share in his sufferings, and to be like him in his death, **3:11** and so, somehow, to attain to the resurrection from the dead.

**3:12** Not that I have already attained this—that is, I have not already been perfected—but I strive to lay hold of that for which Christ Jesus also laid hold of me. **3:13** Brothers and sisters, I do not consider myself to have attained this. Instead I am single-minded: Forgetting the things that are behind and reaching out for the things that are ahead, **3:14** with this goal in mind, I strive toward the prize of the upward call of God in Christ Jesus. **3:15** Therefore let those of us who are "perfect" embrace this point of view. If you think otherwise, God will reveal to you the error of your ways. **3:16** Nevertheless, let us live up to the standard that we have already attained.

**3:17** Be imitators of me, brothers and sisters, and watch carefully those who are living this way, just as you have us as an example. **3:18** For many live, about whom I have often told you, and exult in their shame, and they think about earthly things. **3:20** But our citizenship is in heaven—and we also await a savior from there, the Lord Jesus Christ, **3:21** who will transform these humble bodies of ours into the likeness of his glorious body by means of that power by which he is able to subject all things to himself.

**4:1** So then, my brothers and sisters, dear friends whom I long to see, my joy and crown, stand in the Lord in this way, my dear friends!

**4:2** I appeal to Euodia and to Syntyche to agree in the Lord. **4:3** Yes, I say also to you, true companion, help them. They have struggled together in the gospel ministry along with me and Clement and my other coworkers, whose names are in the book of life. **4:4** Rejoice in the Lord always. Again I say, rejoice! **4:5** Let everyone see your gentleness. The Lord is near! **4:6** Do not be anxious about anything. Instead, in every situation, through prayer and petition with thanksgiving, tell your requests to God. **4:7** And the peace of God that surpasses all understanding will guard your hearts and minds in Christ Jesus.

**4:8** Finally, brothers and sisters, whatever is true, whatever is worthy of respect, whatever is just, whatever is pure, whatever is lovely, whatever is commendable, if something is excellent or praiseworthy, think about these things. **4:9** And what you learned and received and heard and saw in me, do these things. And the God of peace will be with you.

**4:10** I have great joy in the Lord because now at last you have again expressed your concern for me. (Now I know you were concerned before but had no opportunity to do anything.) **4:11** I am not saying this because I am in need, for I have learned to be content in any circumstance. **4:12** I have experienced times of need and times of abundance. In any and every circumstance I have learned the secret of contentment, whether I go satisfied or hungry, have plenty or nothing. **4:13** I am able to do all things through the one who strengthens me. **4:14** Nevertheless, you did well to share with me in my trouble.

**4:15** And as you Philippians know, at the beginning of my gospel ministry, when I left Macedonia, no church shared with me in this matter of giving and receiving except you alone. **4:16** For even in Thessalonica on more than one occasion you sent something for my need. **4:17** I do not say this because I am seeking a gift.

Rather, I seek the credit that abounds to your account. **4:18** For I have received everything, and I have plenty. I have all I need because I received from Epaphroditus what you sent—a fragrant offering, an acceptable sacrifice, very pleasing to God. **4:19** And my God will supply your every need according to his glorious riches in Christ Jesus. **4:20** May glory be given to God our Father forever and ever. Amen.

**4:21** Give greetings to all the saints in Christ Jesus. The brothers with me here send greetings. **4:22** All the saints greet you, especially those who belong to Caesar's household. **4:23** The grace of the Lord Jesus Christ be with your spirit.

2. Now that you're finished writing, what did you observe? Any words repeated? Concepts emphasized?

_____

_____

_____

3. What, if anything, struck you as particularly meaningful?

_____

_____

_____

4. Did a particular command bring conviction or example stand out for you to follow? If so, what?

_____

_____

_____

> Finally, my brothers and sisters, rejoice in the Lord! To write this again is no trouble to me, and it is a safeguard for you **(Phil. 3:1)**.

We don't know for certain whether Paul ever returned to Philippi after writing the letter we have just studied. After his death, following a second Roman imprisonment, we hear little of the church or of the town of Philippi until early in the second century. Then Ignatius, bishop of Antioch, was condemned as a Christian and taken to Rome to be thrown to wild beasts. On his way he passed through Philippi, where the

> *Would you like to read Polycarp's Letter to the Philippians? You can find it online here: www.early christianwritings.com/polycarp .html*

believers reportedly showed him affection and care. Afterward he wrote several letters to his fellow bishops, Polycarp being one of them. Polycarp fulfilled Ignatius's request to send his library of letters and took that opportunity at that time (c. A. D. 110–140) to send a letter to the Philippians. It contains encouragement, advice, and warning. And from it we determine that the church was doing well despite the fact that he has to issue a reprimanded to a couple who illicitly profit from the ministry.

We also have a few remaining records of bishops from Philippi, whose names we find listed in decisions of councils held at Sardica (AD 344), Ephesus (431) and Chalcedon (451). And we know that Philippi was nearly destroyed by an earthquake in 619. Experts assume it never fully recovered.

We have no written history of the city's final destruction, but the site has been in ruins for centuries, having been—most likely—finished off by the Turks.

The first archeological description of the city was made in 1856. Then excavations began in 1914, but the World Wars interrupted them. Work resumed, and most of the archeological work there happened between 1920 and 1978.

Philippi's remains, accessible to visitors today, contain striking portions of fortifications, columns and a theater, numerous rock-cut reliefs and inscriptions, as well as parts of a triumphal arch.[18] Perhaps in the next few decades your own study of Philippians will be enhanced as archeologists learn more about the first-century culture there.

Yet while the city of Philippi has been long since abandoned, the eternal work established there two thousand years ago endures. The hospitality of a fabric rep, the testimony of a jailer, the generosity of a church, and the words of a grateful recipient—these are among the many gifts from Philippi that continue to benefit us today.

What are you building that lasts?

**Pray:** *Thank You, Lord, for Your Word. Thank You for the testimony of those who have gone before me who have left their words and their witness to cheer me on in the faith. Thank You for this book of the Bible and the encouragement it provides. Help me to think worthy thoughts, to rejoice always, trusting that You are in control. Help me to pray without ceasing and to know the kind of peace that can be explained only supernaturally. Help me to be gentle, knowing you are near. Help me to pursue Christ as the one true treasure worth giving my life for. In His name I ask these things, Amen.*

### Memorize:
"Rejoice in the Lord always. Again I say, rejoice! Let everyone see your gentleness. The Lord is near! Do not be anxious about anything. Instead, in every situation, through prayer and petition with thanksgiving, tell your requests to God. And the peace of God that surpasses all understanding will guard your hearts and minds in Christ Jesus.

Finally, brothers and sisters, whatever is true, whatever is worthy of respect, whatever is just, whatever is pure, whatever is lovely, whatever is commendable, if something is excellent or praiseworthy, think about these things. And what you learned and received and heard and saw in me, do these things. And the God of peace will be with you." (Phil. 4:4–9)

[18] ISBE, CD-ROM version, "Philippi."

# LEADER'S GUIDE

## QUALIFICATIONS

Begin with prayer, asking the Lord to guide you. Do you sense God leading you to facilitate a group? To direct a Coffee Cup Bible study, you do not need to have a seminary degree, be a public speaker, or even possess the spiritual gift of teaching. You need only to have a desire to see people grow through God's Word and a genuine concern for their spiritual growth. Often the person best suited to the facilitator's role is not someone who likes to impart knowledge (teach). Rather, it's someone who enjoys drawing out others and hearing *them* talk (encouragement).

## GETTING STARTED

Pray about whom you should invite to join you. Then begin inviting participants and set a deadline for commitments. Ask yourself the best way to communicate to others the opportunity for group study—Church bulletin? Web site? Blog? Text? Email? Flier? Poster? Phone call?

If you envision a church-sponsored study with a number of small groups, aim to give participants at least several months' notice so you can schedule a room and so participants can add the event to their calendars. Enlist the help of the appropriate church servants to work out details relating to time and place.

If you plan to gather a small group of friends, decide as a group the best time and place to meet. Ideally small groups should be limited to about eight to ten members.

Take book orders, collect payment, and distribute books in advance or have each individual take care of obtaining her own. The former is recommended, however, as bulk discounts are often available, and people are more likely to follow through with attending if they have a study in hand.

Before your first Bible discussion time, hold a kick-off brunch or get your group together at church, a coffee shop, or in a home. Pray for each person who will be attending, requesting God's presence and that each would have a desire to learn the Word. Open with prayer.

Provide opportunities for members to get acquainted if they don't already know each other. Do this by providing introductions or offering some ice-breaker questions that include each participant giving her name and some background information. Ask a benign question with the potential for humor such as "What is your favorite household appliance" (Water heater? Blender? Coffee maker?). This will help people open up to each other. One artist-led group asked this question and provided Play-Doh so each participant could make an image of her appliance, and others had to guess what it was.

You will need to determine before this meeting whether to distribute study books in advance or to hand them out at this event. You also need to decide if members should read only the introduction the first week, or if they are to read both the introduction and complete the first week of study. If the former, plan for how you will fill the time at your first meeting, as you will have little to discuss. (Perhaps you can do a service project together, such as writing to a child whom a group member sponsors. Or share your own faith-story, so your group can get to know you.) Something else you'll need to determine—do you want to complete each chapter in one week, or do you want to spread your study out over an eight-week period? If the latter, determine where to divide the book for each week's study.

Obtain permission to distribute contact information among the members or consider setting up a social network page for your group. Include phone, email, and street address information.

## Your First Discussion Meeting

When the group meets for the first discussion, be sure all participants meet each other, if they haven't already. Distribute contact information, and be sure everyone has a study handy.

You will spend most of your time in discussion. If your group
members hardly know each other or seem reluctant to talk, use an ice-
breaker question to get them started. Try to come up with something
that relates to the topic without requiring a spiritual answer. You may
have people in your group who are completely uncomfortable talking
about spiritual things, and the ice breaker is a way to help them participate in a way that's less threatening. In fact for these reasons you
might want to include an ice breaker at the beginning of each discussion to get lighthearted conversation going. See the list of suggestions
below for each week's possible questions.

## Your Weekly Meeting

Begin each session with prayer, and do your best to start on time,
depending on the formality of the group. Set a clear ending time, and
respect participants' schedules.

After prayer, ask the icebreaker question, if you plan to use one.
Then move to discussion. Plan to allow about 45 minutes for this
time. Select the questions you'll ask by going back through the lesson
for the week and choosing about seven open-ended questions. You
can simply circle in your guide the questions you want to ask. Be sure
at least one of your choices covers what you feel is the most important
point from the text for that week.

Be careful not to dominate as the leader. Your job is not to instruct
but to draw out. If you have a member who rarely says anything, periodically direct an easy question specifically to her.

When you finish the final question, ask members if they want to
share prayer requests, items for thanksgiving, or announcements. Be
sure each prayer request is actually prayed over, and encourage the
group to refrain from answering such requests with advice or related
stories (e.g., "I know someone else with that kind of cancer and she
used an herbal supplement").

When you're finished, be sure each person knows the next assignment as well as the meeting time and place for your next study.

Between meetings, pray for participants. It will mean a lot if you follow up with a phone call, particularly when people have shared urgent requests.

## ICE BREAKERS

*Week 1.* The text for week one focuses on Paul's entire letter and on unity in diversity. So you could ask "What's the most surprising piece of mail you've ever received?" Or if members already know each other well, you could ask a more intense question such as, "Share a time when you witnessed an incidence of racial prejudice."

*Week 2.* The text for the week is about joy in response to the furtherance of the gospel. You could ask members to describe moments when they experienced joy. You'll also be talking about grace. So you could open with, "What is the kindest thing a stranger has ever done for you?" Or because you'll be discussing the Body of Christ using the metaphors of brother and sister, you could ask each member of your group to tell whether she has any siblings and a little bit about them.

*Week 3.* The subject for week three is Jesus' humility. You could begin with a question such as "Share a time when you thought someone was really humble." Or you could ask the opposite—about someone they thought was proud, as long as nobody gives names. If the group seems more comfortable being vulnerable, you can help them distinguish between humiliation and humility by asking, "What's one of the dumbest things you've ever done?" You as the leader will set the stage for how open members are with their faults. If you go first and share your foibles, they will be more inclined to do likewise.

*Week 4.* In week four you'll study Paul's use of an athletic metaphor. To tie in your ice breaker with the lesson this week, you could open by asking members to tell their favorite Olympic events, memorable moments, and top-pick athletes. In his epistle to the Philippians, Paul also brought up frequently the issue of citizenship. So you could ask what participants like best about their country of origin.

*Week 5.* During the fifth week of study, you'll focus on being content. So have participants tell about a time when they felt totally content. Remember that these ice breaker questions are simply to get discussion started, by opening with an easy question for which everyone should be able to give an answer without feeling intimidated. Feel free to craft questions that better fit your own group.

## More than Bible Study

Perhaps you would like to combine your time in Bible study with service. You can choose one of the following ways or come up with your own.

Have each person bring something every week to donate. One week, they can bring used eyeglasses. The next, cell phones to recycle. Then used Bibles to go to an organization that distributes them to the needy or in countries where Bibles are not readily available. And finally, books to donate to the public library or your church library. Other possibilities are combining your time with a "baby shower" to benefit a Pregnancy Resource Center. Or assembling Christmas boxes for Samaritan's Purse. You can involve the group in deciding what they want to do.

Combine your study with your church's missionary needs. One week have everyone bring supplies for someone's mission trip such as power bars, dried soup, seeds. Often short-term teams need items to give to translators as gifts as well as VBS prizes. My congregation's sister-church in Mexico sometimes asks for school supplies in September. Missionaries in Mexico ask for Spanish Bibles. You could ask your congregation's web master to set up an Amazon Associates' account with a link through your church's web pages, and direct all members to order through the link. Choose a mission to benefit from all proceeds. Yet another possibility is bringing office and bathroom supplies for your church.

Target a people group to learn about and pray for as part of your time together.

"Adopt" a missionary of the week/month to pray for and to learn about each time you meet.

Choose a group within your community to serve. If a nursing home, volunteer together one week. If the local homeless shelter, donate pillow cases. Or learn to knit and send scarves in the winter. If your local fire fighters need your support, take cookies. Volunteer to pick up trash in an area where your city has a need.

By linking time in God's Word with time serving others, you will help group members move from compartmentalizing to integrating their discipleship time and the stewardship of their resources.

Lists of and links to additional helps for your Bible discussion time are available at www.aspire2.com in the Coffee Cup Bible Study section of the site. If your group generates ideas they want to share with others, send them through the contact page on the aspire2 web site. We'd love to know what ideas worked for you!

Perhaps you have some artists in your group who need more right-brained interaction. Songs, jewelry, paintings, photos, collages, poetry, prayers, psalms—the options for creative interaction in response to the truths learned in Philippians are endless. Remember that examples of others' creations made in conjunction with Bible study are available in the galleries at www.soulpersuit.com.

God bless you as you serve the Body of Christ in this way!

**Other Books in the Coffee Cup Bible Study Series®**

## About the NET BIBLE®

The NET BIBLE® is an exciting new translation of the Bible with 60,932 translators' notes! These translators' notes make the original Greek, Hebrew and Aramaic texts of the Bible far more accessible and unlocks the riches of the Bible's truth from entirely new perspectives.

The NET BIBLE® is the first modern Bible to be completely free for anyone, anywhere in the world to download as part of a powerful new "Ministry First" approach being pioneered at bible.org.

**Download the entire NET Bible and
60,932 notes for free at www.bible.org**

*Trustworthy Bible Study Resources™*

## About the bible.org ministry

Before there was eBay® . . . before there was Amazon.com® . . . there was bible.org! Bible.org is a non-profit (501c3) Christian ministry headquartered in Dallas, Texas. In the last decade bible.org has grown to serve millions of individuals around the world and provides thousands of trustworthy resources for Bible study (2 Tim 2:2).

**Go to www.bible.org for thousands
of trustworthy resources including:**

- The NET BIBLE®
- Discipleship Materials
- The Theology Program
- More than 10,000 Sermon Illustrations
- ABC's of Christian Growth
- Bible Dictionaries and Commentaries